Shakespeare
and His Theatre

Shakespeare
and His Theatre

by

Gerald Eades Bentley

UNIVERSITY OF NEBRASKA PRESS
LINCOLN AND LONDON

Portions of this book originally were presented in the Montgomery Lectureship on Contemporary Civilization at the University of Nebraska.

Copyright © 1964 by the University of Nebraska Press
All Rights Reserved
Library of Congress Catalog card number 64-11350
International Standard Book Number 0-8032-0220-2
First Landmark Edition Printing: 1976
Most recent printing indicated by first digit below:
3 4 5 6 7 8 9 10

Manufactured in the United States of America

PREFACE

Each of the chapters in this volume was originally prepared to be delivered, in one form or another, as a public lecture. They were presented to audiences at the University of Nebraska, at the Elizabethan Club of Yale, at the University of Cincinnati, at the University of Leicester, and at the International Shakespeare Conference, or the School of Elizabethan Studies, both at Stratford-upon-Avon. Though no chapter appears in its original form, all of them envisage an attentive audience, not isolated scholars: the examples are deliberately selected as familiar, not obscure ones; the documentation is minimal; and the style is more colloquial than precise.

CONTENTS

I. SHAKESPEARE AND THE READERS OF HIS PLAYS 1

II. SHAKESPEARE AND HIS DRAMATIC COMPANY 27

III. SHAKESPEARE AND THE GLOBE THEATRE 47

IV. SHAKESPEARE AND THE BLACKFRIARS THEATRE 65

V. SHAKESPEARE'S THEATRE AND AFTER 101

I.

Shakespeare and the Readers of His Plays

IN THE Shakespeare publications of the last thirty years there have been many studies which concentrate largely on imagery and word patterns in the plays—studies of figures of speech, of iterative images, of subtle word connotations, of dominant metaphors, of poetic symbols—all of which are interpreted as evidence of Shakespeare's attempts to suggest this or that to the *readers* of his plays. Since 1925 or 1930, there have probably been more Shakespearean studies of this sort than of any other kind—studies by Miss Caroline Spurgeon, by G. Wilson Knight, by William Empson, by Wolfgang Clemen, by Cleanth Brooks, Robert Heilman and a host of others. In the Shakespeare Industry, as Ivor Brown once called it, the factory with an output which even the Russians would envy is the factory called Shakespeare's Imagery.

Now all these fascinating studies of images, poetic symbols, and word patterns require a very careful and sensitive reading of the plays. Even a thoughtful and uninterrupted examination of the text from Act I, scene i to the end of the play is generally not enough to understand the points made by so much modern criticism about the play; one must work backward and forward through the comedy or tragedy—from Act I to Act III, from Act IV back to Act II, from the climax back to the opening, from the denoument back to the rising action. Even the most perceptive playgoer could never take in these verbal patterns by the ear alone, and the students of imagery do not maintain that he could. They are studying Shakespeare the Poet, rather than Shakespeare the Playwright. They take for granted Shakespeare's interest in the *readers* of his plays; some of the more intense of these critics seem tacitly to assume Shakespeare's almost exclusive interest in readers. And these assumptions lead one to inquire "How much interest did Shakespeare really have in the readers of his plays?" Or, if we are to use a scholar's methods rather than those of a writer of popular fiction, "What evidence exists of Shakespeare's interest in the readers of his plays?"

One always takes it for granted that a poet is interested in preparing his compositions to be read, and there is a tendency to think of Shakespeare as a Renaissance poet, in much the same category as Edmund Spenser and John Milton. It seems obvious that poetry was written to be read—at least in the five hundred years since printing became common. But suppose we question the general assumption, and look for the evidence. Such evidence is easy enough to find for Spenser and Milton. Both of them, like many other poets of their time, wrote dedications and prefaces and explanatory statements for their publications. Their own statements about their poems are found in letters which they wrote to friends about literary problems and about their own publications. Not only Spenser and Milton, but most of the other poets of the time either published statements about their poetry or left statements in manuscript letters or comments showing their interest in getting their works into the hands of readers and having them understood.

But no such evidence exists for a single one of Shakespeare's thirty-eight plays. No play of his, printed during his lifetime, had a dedication, or an author's preface, or an address to the reader. There is no known comment in print or in manuscript made by Shakespeare on any of his plays. None of them ever appeared in print with anything which could be attributed to Shakespeare except the bare speeches of the characters themselves; a few stage directions—far too few for readers—and five prologues and six epilogues out of the fifty or more prologues and epilogues which these plays presumably had originally.

It is sometimes suggested that the bareness of the published texts of the plays is simply an indication that he was writing plays, not lyric poetry or epic poetry like Milton or Spenser whose writings were prepared solely for readers and not (like plays) prepared primarily for an audience. Now there is point in this distinction between plays and nondramatic poetry; it is easy to forget that lyric poets always have readers directly in mind as they write—they are *communicating to readers.* Playwrights, on the other hand, must always have an audience in a theatre as their first consideration; readers usually come later, if at all.

Since this normal concern of a dramatist with an audience rather than with readers is well known, it is sometimes suggested that *any* dramatist in the time of Elizabeth and James I would ignore readers just as Shakespeare did. But this is not true. Many Elizabethan dramatists did not ignore readers. Thomas Dekker wrote an address "To all good Fellows, Professors of the Gentle Craft" for the first edition of his *The Shoemakers' Holiday* in the same year that *Henry V, Henry IV,* Part 2, *Much Ado about Nothing, A Midsummer Night's Dream,* and *The Merchant of Venice* were printed with no comment from Shakespeare. John Marston wrote dedications and addresses to the readers of his plays *The Malcontent* and *Antonio and Mellida,* and Thomas Middleton wrote an Epistle to the Readers for his play *The Family of Love* in the same years that *The Merry Wives of Windsor, Hamlet,* and *King Lear* came from the London presses with no comment whatever from their author. Ben Jonson prepared dedications and addresses to the readers, and he solicited commendatory verses from his friends for the editions of *Sejanus, Volpone, Catiline,* and *The Alchemist* in about the same years. Chapman and Heywood and Field and Daborne, and Shakespeare's collaborator John Fletcher, all wrote dedications and addresses to readers for several of their plays, as did many of the lesser known dramatists of the reigns of Elizabeth and James.[1]

All these examples of introductory material published with the original editions of Elizabethan plays constitute good evidence that these eight or nine Elizabethan dramatists certainly hoped to have their plays read; and they took occasion to speak to their readers when the plays came into print. All the plays I have mentioned were published in London during Shakespeare's lifetime. So it cannot be truthfully said that the publication of plays with bare, unadorned texts like Shakespeare's was standard practice in the period: Dekker, Marston, Middleton, Jonson, Chapman, Heywood, Field, Daborne, and Fletcher all showed their interest in readers by writing dedications, prefaces, and addresses to readers to be published with the texts of the plays. But Shakespeare never did.

There is another peculiarity of the quarto editions of Shakespeare's plays published during his

---

[1] Such general statements about play publication can be most easily checked or supplemented from the transcriptions and appendices in W. W. Greg, *A Bibliography of the English Printed Drama to the Restoration* (4 vols.; London, 1939–1959).

lifetime which shows the same lack of concern for readers. The simplest service any dramatist or editor can perform in preparing the text of a play for publication is to collect the names of the characters and print them before the first entrance for the assistance of readers. Such dramatis personae appear at the beginning of many Elizabethan play quartos—indeed, in a majority of those published after the year 1600. But not a single quarto for a play of Shakespeare's published in the poet's lifetime has a dramatis personae. Moreover, not a single one of Shakespeare's quartos is divided into acts and scenes for the convenience of the reader, though many of the quartos of other dramatists are so divided.

What is the meaning of this peculiar bareness of the early quarto editions of Shakespeare's plays? Sometimes it is suggested that Shakespeare—like a few other great artists—wanted his plays to be read but would not toady to the reading public. People who find such a man attractive suggest that Shakespeare was the kind of personality who was confident in his own art, and who disdained to make any effort to get a favorable hearing for it. Such people like to imagine Shakespeare saying what his friend, the dramatist Ben Jonson, actually *did* say at the end of the epilogue of his comedy *Cynthia's Revels* in 1601. As the last line of this epilogue Ben Jonson wrote:

> By God, 'tis good. And if you like 't, you may.

I rather like this attitude myself. But for the historic Shakespeare it will not do. If one considers the evidence and not one's own imagination, it is perfectly clear that William Shakespeare was not that kind of a man. For though he never used prefaces, dedications, or addresses to the reader for his *plays,* he did use them when he published nondramatic verse—*Venus and Adonis* and *The Rape of Lucrece.* Both these poems were published with dedications to the Earl of Southampton, dedications signed by William Shakespeare. These two dedications to Southampton show clearly that Shakespeare was not averse to addressing a nobleman at the beginning of a work; he did it for his two narrative poems. But he never did it for a single play. To me these facts suggest that Shakespeare was interested in readers for his poems, but that he was not interested in readers for his plays.

But such readers are reluctant to believe that Shakespeare showed no interest in them. They sometimes argue that Shakespeare's interest in readers must be demonstrated by the fact that his plays, after all, did get published; if he was really uninterested in readers, surely the plays would never have been printed at all.

Now this argument sounds convincing (like so many popular arguments) until you begin to examine the first editions of the plays. Then one finds that the texts of the plays, when they are all considered together, seem to show precisely the opposite. They show an author curiously uninterested in readers.

During the last two centuries a huge volume of critical literature has been devoted to the multitudinous problems of Shakespeare's text, and many of the problems have not yet received a generally recognized solution. But the descriptive and enumerative task has now been pretty well accomplished, and the general character of the first editions of the plays are known to all interested scholars. Note what these characteristics imply about Shakespeare's own part in the publication of his plays.

The generally accepted canon of the poet's dramatic work is the thirty-six plays which were published by his actor-friends and associates, John Heminges and Henry Condell, in the First Folio seven years after his death, plus two others unaccountably omitted, *Pericles* and *The Two Noble Kinsmen*. Of these thirty-eight plays, eighteen were given to readers for the first time in 1623, and a nineteenth, *The Two Noble Kinsmen*, in 1634. One other play, though it was published for the second time in the folio, had been first printed in the preceding year, 1622, six years after Shakespeare's death. Thus there are twenty of his plays which the author could never have seen in print. All the evidence we possess seems to show that he cared little whether readers ever saw them or not. For all the effort Shakespeare ever made, these plays might have been only names to modern readers—like so many hundreds of other lost plays of the time. And these twenty plays, unpublished in Shakespeare's lifetime, are not youthful indiscretions which he might have wished to suppress for artistic reasons—as Ben Jonson suppressed his own early indiscretions like *Hot Anger Soon Cooled*, and *Richard Crookback*. The plays which Shakespeare never saw in print include such masterpieces as *Macbeth, As You Like It, Julius Caesar, The Tempest, Twelfth Night, Antony and Cleopatra,* and *Othello*. So far as Shakespeare knew when he died, these plays would never be read except by actors learning their roles. It is difficult to find any evidence of interest in readers here.

What about the eighteen other plays of the accepted canon? What do the texts of these plays show about Shakespeare's interest in readers?

Three of the plays printed in quarto in Shakespeare's lifetime appeared in such a mangled form as to be only partially intelligible, and these three were not printed in a more correct form until they appeared in the folio of 1623, seven years after Shakespeare's death. The three are *The Merry Wives of Windsor, Henry VI,* Part 2, and *Henry VI,* Part 3. Not only is each of them badly mutilated, but about 1,000 lines of the text of each is missing. Yet these so called Bad Quartos[2] are all that Shakespeare could ever have seen in print of *The Merry Wives* and the last two parts of *Henry VI.* There is no evidence that he ever made any attempt to get them printed in a decent form. Surely the texts of these three cannot be thought to show an author's concern that his plays be properly understood by *readers.*

---

[2] There are, of course, other Bad Quartos, most notably the first editions of *Hamlet, Romeo and Juliet,* and *Henry V.* But better editions of these three plays did appear before Shakespeare's death.

The other fifteen plays available to readers during Shakespeare's lifetime appeared in varying degrees of completeness. Some, like *Love's Labours Lost* and *Much Ado about Nothing,* are printed about as well as they are in the folio. Others, like *King Lear,* are full of egregious blunders. But all the quartos which appeared in Shakespeare's lifetime have certain characteristics in common, good quartos and bad. None has any list of dramatis personae. None has any act and scene division. All have so many mistakes in character names, in exits and entrances, in spelling and punctuation, so many wrongly assigned speeches and nonsense words that it is impossible to believe that any author has prepared a careful reading text for the printer to use, or that any author has ever read proof as the sheets came from the press.

Many theories have been presented by different textual scholars as to the kind of text the printer had when he set up particular quartos. Evidently different kinds of texts were used for different plays, though there is not yet complete agreement as to the character of the particular manuscript used in each individual case. But, so far as I know, no reputable scholar of the last twenty-five years has ever contended that any quarto was set up from a manuscript carefully prepared by Shakespeare as a readers' text, or that Shakespeare himself ever carefully read proof on any of them.

Could it be that Shakespeare really did have readers in mind when he prepared his plays, but that his was a genius temperamentally incapable of spending itself on the grinding drudgery of carefully prepared printer's copy and conscientious proof reading? Genius of this type often makes a strong appeal to young readers, who are inclined to think that their own assigned chores are just such drudgery. True enough, such writers can sometimes be found. Shakespeare, however, was not one of them. This assertion is a safe one because we do have two examples of his work which *were* carefully prepared for readers and which must have been proof read. They show that he did submit himself to drudgery when he thought it important. The two examples, however, are poems, not plays. *Venus and Adonis* and *The Rape of Lucrece* were intended for readers, and they were prepared for publication by Shakespeare himself, as his signature to the dedications shows.

These two long poems exhibit Shakespeare's treatment of his text when he was interested in readers; they are as clean texts as any Elizabethan literary publication. Most scholars have concluded that such a correct text could result only from a manuscript carefully prepared by Shakespeare and proof read by him as well.

The difference between the accuracy of the texts of the poems and the gross inaccuracy of the texts of all the play quartos is striking. Note how striking. In the 1,194 lines of *Venus and Adonis* there are only two clear errors—errors which have been recognized as such by practically all editors of the poem; in the 1,855 lines of *The Rape of Lucrece* there are only three: a rate of about one and two-thirds errors per 1,000 lines.[3] The errors in the play quartos are almost too numerous to count this way. There would be hundreds, and many of them more serious than the five found in the poems. To get some sort of comparison, I took one of the best quartos, that of *Henry IV,* Part 1, and I began counting errors—not just my idea of an error, but errors which the Variorum edition of the plays shows that most editors since the seventeenth century have recognized. In the first hundred lines of

[3] The errors and the general recognition of them can be fairly easily checked from *A New Variorum Edition of Shakespeare: The Poems,* ed. Hyder Edward Rollins (Philadelphia and London, 1938).

the play there were sixteen such errors. That is, the rate of error in one of the very best quartos is about one hundred sixty per 1,000 lines, or at a rate of about one hundred times that in the poems which Shakespeare prepared for readers.

These errors which appear in the quartos Shakespeare might have seen are often not simple transposed letters or bungled punctuation. Many of them would have brought any author up short, though they could pass a sleepy proofreader. For instance, in corrected texts of *Troilus and Cressida* the exchange between Andromache and Cassandra in Act V, scene iii, lines 19–23 reads:

Andromache.
  O, be persuaded! Do not count it holy
  To hurt by being just. It is as lawful,
  For we would give much, to use violent thefts
  And rob in the behalf of charity.
Cassandra.
  It is the purpose that makes strong the vow,

But in the only printed version Shakespeare could have seen, three lines have been dropped and the two speeches run together so that what was written as an exchange reads:

Andromache.
  O be persuaded, do not count it holy,

It is the purpose that makes strong the vow,

Even worse is a passage in *King Lear*. Where we read in Act IV, scene i, of Edgar's horrified sight of his blinded father:

> Enter *Gloucester*, led by an *Old Man*.
> But who comes here?
> My father, poorly led?

the original quarto gives Edgar's query several lines before the entrance, and the speech reads:

> Who's here, my father parti, eyd....

It seems unlikely that any author could have passed over errors so gross as these.

Now what can we conclude from this inquiry into the state of Shakespeare's text? We set out to find what information the general character of the dramatist's text might convey about Shakespeare's attitude toward readers. The answer seems fairly clear.

The texts suggest that Shakespeare obviously had readers in mind when he wrote his poems and that he consequently prepared careful texts for the publishers. But in the case of his *plays* the conclusion must be entirely different. Since, at the time of his death, half his plays had never appeared in print at all, and since there is no mention of manuscripts in his will, and no evidence of any action about them taken by his executors or beneficiaries, we must conclude that he was indifferent as to whether half his plays ever reached readers. And for the other half, the eighteen plays which did get printed before 1616, the character of the quarto texts suggest no interest at all in readers by the greatest English poet.

Such conclusions are not popular, but it seems to me they are inescapable. Modern critics and scholars do not so much *deny* them as *ignore* them. They seldom assert that Shakespeare's plays were carefully prepared for readers, but how many critics tacitly assume that they were, and then go on to analyze diction and imagery for appeals which could be made only to readers and which no audience in the theatre could ever catch! How many critical studies of the last thirty years ignore the theatre and discuss Shakespeare's art wholly in terms of poetical appeals to readers!

Many people have noticed that there is one group of nineteenth- and twentieth-century writers which does not ignore these conclusions about Shakespeare to be drawn from the state of his text. The members of this group talk constantly of the fact that half of the plays were first printed after Shakespeare's death, and the fact that none of the quartos printed in his lifetime received the careful preparation for the reader which Edmund Spenser gave to the first three books of *The Faerie Queene* or Milton to the first edition of *Paradise Lost*. They face the facts about William Shakespeare and the state of the text honestly enough, and they insist on a conclusion which to them seems obvious, namely that William Shakespeare could not have been the author of the masterpieces printed under his name. At this point, of course, there is wild disagreement as to what author really did write them —whether Francis Bacon, or the Earl of Derby, or the Earl of Southampton, or Sir Edward Dyer, or Christopher Marlowe, or Queen Elizabeth, or a nun named Anne Whatley.[4]

No experienced literary scholar has ever been taken in by these fantastic theories, but too few people note what is really wrong with the arguments. The anti-Stratfordians do face the facts con-

[4] The numerous anti-Stratfordian theories are well summarized by Frank W. Wadsworth, *The Poacher from Stratford: A Partial Account of the Controversy over the Authorship of Shakespeare's Plays* (Berkeley and Los Angeles, 1958).

cerning the publication of Shakespeare's plays, but they go sadly astray in *explaining* the situation, because they are ignorant, or very ill-informed, concerning the environment in which Shakespeare or any other Elizabethan dramatist lived and worked. They postulate situations and attitudes which are common enough in the nineteenth and twentieth centuries but which were impossible or unknown in the sixteenth century. The general principle of literary understanding and interpretation which the anti-Stratfordians have violated is a fundamental one, though it is sometimes belittled nowadays.

The principle is that to understand Shakespeare, or any other artist, his work must be considered in the historical environment in which his creative genius operated. It is painful to note how frequently this principle has been ignored by literary critics and historians—and to what cost! Many of the absurdities of Shakespeare criticism have been the result. Our Victorian great-grandparents wanted to think of Shakespeare not as an Elizabethan, but as a Victorian. To many of them he was Alfred Lord Tennyson with a somewhat shorter beard. Even worse, they tried to eliminate from his plays those passages which Lord Tennyson would never have written, and the textual critics explained that the normal Elizabethan bawdry found in most of Shakespeare's plays must have been inserted by those nasty men, the actors.

And how often these solemn Victorians spoiled Shakespeare's carefully planned effect by their expurgating! For instance, in *The Merchant of Venice* Shakespeare carefully builds up the rejoicing at the planned marriages of Portia and Bassanio and Nerissa and Gratiano in the middle of the third act, after the choice of the caskets. It is important to develop the rejoicing and the gaiety, because the shocking news of Antonio's arrest and danger of death are planned to break in upon them when the messenger arrives from Venice. Betrothal rejoicings were standard in Elizabethan England; and as in so many countries, a few bawdy insinuations were the normal accompaniment whether the bride were a dairy maid or a princess. In the play, Gratiano announces to the happy Bassanio that he and Nerissa are to be married also. Bassanio replies:

Bassanio.
  Our feast shall be much honoured in your marriage.
Gratiano.
  [*to Nerissa*] We'll play with them the first boy

for a thousand ducats.
Nerissa.
What, and stake down?
Gratiano.
No, we shall ne'er win at that sport, and stake down.

Now the Victorians were shocked at this and cut it out of the play, claiming it to be an insertion by those wicked actors. But their real reason for thinking so was *assumed,* not stated—namely that Tennyson could never have written such a passage, and therefore Shakespeare never did.

But are we so very different in our enlightened twentieth century? Do our critics ever try to remold Shakespeare in the image of our own admired favorite? I suggest that you reread some of the Shakespeare criticism of the last three or four decades, and then ask yourself whether the critic was really thinking of William Shakespeare, the actor-dramatist, or was he imagining T. S. Eliot in doublet and hose. The old principle of sound criticism is still valid. To understand any artist, his work must be considered in the historical environment in which his genius operated.

But there is a corollary principle which seems to me equally valid, and which is even more commonly ignored, especially in studies of the work of William Shakespeare. This corollary principle is that to understand the work of Shakespeare, or any other artist, his works must be considered in the *professional* environment in which his genius operated. For Shakespeare this professional environment was the London professional theatre. And here the difficulty for so many critics and readers arises, for the stage of a sixteenth-century theatre is a much less familiar place than the study of nondramatic poets like Spenser or Milton. How devilishly tempting it is to take William Shakespeare out of that strange and difficult place, the green room of the Globe theatre, in that London red light district, the Bankside, and then surreptitiously deposit him in Milton's study at Horton! Then when he is safely and securely deposited at Horton we can all watch him develop themes and use erudite sources and spin imagistic patterns and elaborate Christian allegories just as John Milton did. How cozy and comfortable and familiar it is for all teachers and critics and readers of plays! But how exquisitely uncomfortable for William Shakespeare! For Shakespeare (unlike all other English poets of prominence with whom we are more at ease) was essentially a man of the theatre, not a man of the study.

The genius of this man is so unparalleled that we too often tend to think of him as one apart, but when we do associate him with a group, it is with the Elizabethan dramatists. The others of the group we think of primarily as playwrights; Shakespeare is the only one whose work is commonly wrenched out of its proper professional environment and treated without reference to the theatre—as if he had written for readers. This is ironic, for of all the group of Elizabethan dramatists Shakespeare's connection with the theatre was not the slightest—it was the most complete. He was not an amateur dramatist like some of the group—John Lyly, or Francis Beaumont, or John Ford, or Thomas Lodge. Shakespeare was not even a semi-professional like Thomas Nash or George Chapman or Ben Jonson. He was completely professional. He made his living wholly from the theatre as did the other professionals, Thomas Heywood, James Shirley, Richard Brome, William Rowley, and Nathan Field.

Now all professional dramatists of Shakespeare's time were more closely associated with their theatres and actors than modern dramatists are. But there was one group among them which was still more closely linked with the actors. These few Elizabethan professional dramatists were themselves actors in the companies for which they wrote. The best known of these actor-dramatists are Thomas Heywood, Rowley, Field, and Shakespeare.

Even in this highly professional group one man stands out as being most completely identified with one company and its theatres. Rowley and Field shifted their allegiance from troupe to troupe; Heywood even deserted the stage for the last ten or fifteen years of his career. Only Shakespeare of all known Elizabethan and Jacobean dramatists sticks to one company throughout his known career, devoting all his energies to the productions of the most distinguished and most successful acting troupe in London—the Lord Chamberlain-King's company.

Surely William Shakespeare was above all a man of the theatre. No other great English dramatist— not Dryden or Congreve or Sheridan or Shaw—was as independent of readers or as fully occupied with the theatre as Shakespeare was. Two of his narrative poems (written when the London theatres were closed because of plague) were clearly prepared for readers and carefully published, but the bulk of his great achievement, the plays of the First Folio, were just as clearly prepared for the theatre, and I can find no evidence in the editions of these plays published during Shakespeare's lifetime that he gave any consideration to readers at all.

His known career (and it is easy to forget that the life of Shakespeare, which seems so shadowy, can be better documented than that of any other Elizabethan playwright with the possible exception of Ben Jonson) shows a similar concentration on theatre audiences and theatre affairs and not on readers and publishers. At the beginning of his writing career the first reference we have to him is in a theatrical context—Robert Greene's statement about a "tiger's heart wrapped in a player's hide." And at the end of his career we have his last known words in his will, leaving final remembrances to the men long associated with him in the theatrical enterprises at the Globe and the Blackfriars, John Heminges, Henry Condell, and Richard Burbage, his fellow actors of a quarter of a century's dramatic partnership.

It seems to me that this accumulated evidence all points in the same direction. All teachers and critics ought to cling painfully to the central concept that William Shakespeare was essentially a man of the theatre and not a poet writing for readers. Does not the evidence suggest that if we seek the truth (and not the exercise of our own best developed skills) we ought to question the relevance of Shakespeare criticism which ignores the theatres and insists on the importance of recondite patterns of word play inaudible to the ear of any audience? Must we not honestly face our own circumscribed positions as readers and struggle to create a theatrical context as we read?

Shakespeare was himself an actor. He knew something of the melancholy fact that the art of the greatest actor is an ephemeral thing. Perhaps he had something of our difficulty in mind when he wrote the famous passage in his last play:

> Our revels now are ended. These our actors,
> As I foretold you, were all spirits and
> Are melted into air, into thin air;
> And, like the baseless fabric of this vision,
> The cloud-capp'd towers, the gorgeous palaces,
> The solemn temples, the great globe itself,
> Yea, all which it inherit, shall dissolve,
> And, like this insubstantial pageant faded,
> Leave not a rack behind. We are such stuff
> As dreams are made on, and our little life
> Is rounded with a sleep.

II.

Shakespeare and His Dramatic Company

I HAVE TRIED to demonstrate that it is a mistake to examine the plays of Shakespeare as if he had taken great care to prepare a text for readers. Other favorite writers of the English Renaissance—Spenser and Milton and Donne—certainly did write with readers primarily, if not exclusively, in mind. For them our favorite mid-twentieth-century methods of critical analysis may be entirely appropriate. Though the conclusions of such critical examinations may sometimes be preposterous, the methods themselves are suitable for the elucidation of the works of Spenser and Milton and Donne, who clearly prepared their poetry for readers to experience, text in hand. No matter how active these three men may have been in the administration of Ireland, or in the foreign correspondence of Cromwell's government, or in the pulpit of St. Paul's, their great works, which we cherish today, were planned for thoughtful readers using such aids as are available in libraries. They were poets of the study writing for readers in the study.

Shakespeare, it is true, sometimes wrote as they did. *Venus and Adonis, The Rape of Lucrece,* and *The Sonnets* are poems of the study, and they may be elucidated legitimately and fruitfully by methods appropriate to the critical analysis of *The Faerie Queene, Paradise Lost,* and *The Anniversaries.* But in his greatest work, Shakespeare was not a poet of the study, but a poet of the theatre, and it is in his theatrical environment that his plays can be most appropriately examined.

The theatre in any age is highly conservative, probably more traditional than any other form of artistic endeavor. What the actors and their writers have once found to be effective, they cling to for generations in spite of wars, revolutions, and even the basic alterations of their primary instruments, the acting company and the theatre building. When W. S. Gilbert observed

>That every boy and every gal
> That's born into the world alive

> Is either a little Liberal
> Or else a little Conservative.

he was offering no option to his friends in the theatre. Actors are all born little Conservatives.

Many a phenomenon in the history of the theatre illustrates this intense conservatism of players and playwrights. For centuries after the development of the proscenium arch theatre, actors and dramatists continued to use the aside which had lost its basic effectiveness with the abandonment of the platform stage. For years after the house curtain was invented, plays continued to be written and presented as if there were no physical means for the marking off of one movement of the action from another. As early as 1893 William Poel showed how Elizabethan plays ought to be presented,[1] but even in 1964 most performances do not present them so.

This strong reactionary tendency of the theatre was characteristic of the sixteenth century as it is of the twentieth, and it enveloped Shakespeare as it did all his contemporaries. Traditional assumptions and methods are typical of the theatrical

---

[1] See Robert Speaight, *William Poel and the Elizabethan Revival* (Cambridge, Mass., 1954).

environment in which Shakespeare worked, and because, as we shall notice, he was so fully wrapped up in the theatre as playwright, actor, sharer, and theatre owner, we should expect him to be more familiar with these customs and conventions and more expert in manipulating them than were amateurs like Thomas Lodge or semi-professionals like Ben Jonson.

It is interesting to observe certain of these traditional elements in Shakespeare's environment and to note something of the way in which they shaped the writing of his plays. The most basic one was the professional adult acting company as it existed in London at the end of the sixteenth century and the beginning of the seventeenth. To the best of these companies Shakespeare belonged for more than twenty years, and for it he wrote most, possibly all, of his plays.

The great London acting companies of the reigns of Elizabeth and King James were the direct descendants of the strolling troupes which, for more than a century, had been touring England with small repertories of plays—moralities, interludes, chronicles, and romances—troupes like the ones Shakespeare himself depicted on the stage in the strolling players of *The Taming of the Shrew* and in the visiting troupe which comes to Elsinore in *Hamlet*. The great majority of the plays in their repertories are lost, known to us now only by title or by occasional descriptive allusions. But a certain number are still extant, and though they have little literary interest and consequently have usually been ignored by the critics, they can reveal to the alert historian a great deal about the fundamental methods and assumptions developed by the actors and their writers and carried over by these intensely conservative theatre people into the time of Shakespeare.

Among the most illuminating of such fifteenth- and sixteenth-century plays from the repertories of the touring companies are *Mankind, Enough Is as Good as a Feast, Like Will to Like, The Marriage of Wit and Wisdom, All for Money, Lusty Juventus, Horestes,* and *Cambises*.

None of these plays is a literary masterpiece. Little of their verse is better than hack work; the ideas are banal; they are full of crudity and vulgarity. Readers interested only in the inspiration to be derived from our great drama should sedulously avoid all of them. But for the student who wants to understand the working methods of the great Elizabethan dramatists—of Marlowe and Shakespeare and Heywood and Dekker—these third-rate plays can be eye openers.

Such plays, and a number of others like them, have been examined in an interesting and significant book which appeared recently, a book by David Bevington, entitled *From Mankind to Marlowe*.[2] Mr. Bevington has carefully analyzed the plays of the professional actors for more than a century before the advent of Christopher Marlowe and has demonstrated a structural pattern and a casting method which is strikingly uniform. The plays were clearly written to the needs of the acting troupe.

Now some of this has long been known, for a number of the plays were published in the sixteenth century with charts showing how the parts could be doubled to fit the needs of the normal acting company: *Enough Is as Good as a Feast* has a chart showing how seven actors can play the eighteen roles; *Cambises* has a chart adjusting thirty-eight roles to eight actors; the manuscript of *The Marriage of Wit and Wisdom* shows how six actors can handle the nineteen parts; *Horestes* how six

[2] David M. Bevington, *From Mankind to Marlowe: Growth of Structure in the Popular Drama of Tudor England* (Cambridge, Mass., 1962).

actors may take twenty-seven roles. These charts are not odd adaptations for occasional difficult situations; they are a standard device which sets a pattern for the way a playwright must construct his play if it is to be performed by a professional troupe.

Since the theatre is always traditional and practical, it ought to be no surprise to learn that the old pattern which had been developed in more than a century of acting on the road was not abandoned when certain of the touring troupes grew larger and more successful and, as the Lord Admiral's and the Lord Chamberlain's men, spent most of their time at the new theatres in London. These Elizabethan troupes had more actors, more money, and more plays than their predecessors had enjoyed; in the days of Marlowe and Shakespeare they no longer needed to restrict the available performers to six or eight; but the basic system had not changed.

The most conclusive evidence of the continuing system is to be seen in the seven extant manuscripts or fragments called "Plots." These plots are scenarios and casting charts for plays produced by the Lord Admiral's men, the Lord Strange's men, and the Lord Chamberlain's men, probably at the playhouses called The Theatre and The Curtain. The precise dates of performances are uncertain, but there is enough evidence to show that they were all acted during the first half of Shakespeare's career as actor and dramatist in London. The plots are for the productions of plays called:

>*Fortune's Tennis*, Part 2
>*Troilus and Cressida*
>*The Dead Man's Fortune*
>*The Seven Deadly Sins*, Part 2
>*Frederick and Basilea*
>*The Battle of Alcazar*
>*Tamar Cam*, Part 1

As plays, the pieces are insignificant, and the full texts of all but one of them are lost, but as evidence of the continuation of the old traditional methods by the companies of Shakespeare's time, they are conclusive. These plots are most fully analyzed as manuscripts by Sir Walter Greg in his *Dramatic Documents from the Elizabethan Playhouses*.[3] Mr. Bevington makes full use of them to show how they illustrate the old methods still in practice, only expanded to utilize a somewhat larger number of

[3] W. W. Greg, *Dramatic Documents from the Elizabethan Playhouses: Stage Plots: Actors' Parts: Prompt Books* (2 vols.; Oxford, 1931), I, 1–170.

actors, particularly among the hired men. Bevington goes on to show that even the fiery amateur, Kit Marlowe, conformed to the traditional structure of the old plays of the road companies in the tragedies which astonished London in the late 1580's and early 1590's.

Now William Shakespeare was far more a man of the theatre than Christopher Marlowe; his association with actors and playhouses was longer and far more intimate and varied: a Fellow of the Lord Chamberlain's company was steeped in the methods and traditions of the actors as no Pensioner of Corpus Christi, Cambridge, ever was. Since even Marlowe, as Bevington has shown, worked in terms of the needs and traditions of the acting company, Shakespeare can be expected to be even more professionally oriented.

The salient feature of this professional orientation was the acting company—in Shakespeare's case, the Lord Chamberlain's company, which became the King's company with the accession of James I in 1603. Like all the major adult companies of the time, this troupe was made up of three distinct groups. First, the patented members (often called "fellows" of the company)—senior actors who controlled the organization and whose names, including Shakespeare's, appeared in the royal patent granted by Queen Elizabeth and later confirmed by King James giving them royal permission to act plays at their theatres in London, and ordering all mayors, sheriffs, constables, and others to allow them to act in provincial cities and towns.[4] They were the sharers in the organization who divided the profits, acted the major roles, hired lesser actors, collected fees for performances at court, and wore the royal livery to which they were entitled as Grooms of the Chamber in Ordinary to the King. When Hamlet says to Horatio after the success of the play-within-the-play, "Would not this . . . get me a fellowship in a cry of players, sir?" Horatio replies sourly, "Half a share," referring to the stock in the company owned by these patented members.

The second group in Shakespeare's company was made up of hired men, so called in the documents of the time. These hired men were minor actors and other theatrical functionaries who were paid weekly salaries by the patented members or sharers; they played the parts of court gentlemen, citizens, soldiers—like the senators in *Julius Caesar* and *Othello* or the courtiers in *Hamlet* and *All's Well*.

[4] See below, pp. 52–53.

The hired men were also theatrical functionaries necessary to the running of the Globe or the Theatre—stage keepers, book holders, musicians, box holders, and the like.

The third group in the Lord Chamberlain's men and in other adult acting groups of the time was made up of boys, youngsters of six or eight to eighteen who played the roles of women and children and (at least in the case of one boy actor) the roles of very old men. The boys lived with certain of the major actors as apprentices lived with their masters, and they probably spent all their waking hours either in the theatre or listening to the endless talk of actors about the theatre. It is a great mistake to imagine that these boys were incompetent just because we in the twentieth century are not accustomed to the tradition which they represent. Our usual misconception of the boy actors, and our transfer of our own inadequacies to Shakespeare were eloquently expressed by the great nineteenth-century actress, Helena Faucit. In her book called *On Some of Shakespeare's Female Characters,* Miss Faucit wrote:

> Think of a boy as Juliet! as "heavenly Rosalind!"
> ... How could any youth, however gifted and specially trained, even faintly suggest these fair and

noble women to an audience? Woman's words, woman's thoughts, coming from a man's lips, a man's heart—it is monstrous to think of! One quite pities Shakespeare, who had to put up with seeing his brightest creations thus marred, misrepresented, spoiled."[5]

Miss Faucit's self-praise implied in these remarks about some of her most famous roles may be amusing in its naiveté, but the general attitude expressed is a very common one. It is still a familiar gambit of criticism to transfer one's own prejudices and inadequacies to Shakespeare and then readjust the plays to make them fit.

But the seventeenth-century Englishmen who saw the boys perform detected none of these inadequacies. English travelers, like Thomas Coryate, who went to Italy in Shakespeare's time, wrote back that they saw actresses on the stage in Venice and were surprised to find that they were *as good as* the boy actors back home in London. The poet and dramatist, Ben Jonson, who was not addicted to flattery, wrote a beautiful epitaph on one of these boy actors who died when he was thirteen years old. Jonson said that when the boy died he had

[5] Helena Faucit, Lady Martin, *On Some of Shakespeare's Female Characters* (New Ed.; New York, 1887), p. 4.

already been the "Stage's jewell" in London for three years. Fifty years later one of the theatre prompters in the Restoration, a man who had worked with most of the great actresses of that period, said that he doubted if any of those actresses could equal the boy Edward Kynaston in affecting an audience. Obviously the people who saw them thought the boys better than we can easily imagine.

Such a company—boys, hired men, and sharers—was the organization for which all Shakespeare's plays were written. The poet himself spent all his creative life as a member of such an acting troupe, and he was one of its directors and principal policy makers; however other conditions might change, the general character of the dramatic company for which his plays were prepared did not change. The company is a constant influence in all the comedies and histories and tragedies which came in such abundance from the pen of William Shakespeare. Certain strong and permanent influences of this acting troupe are clearly to be seen in the plays.

Most apparent is the fact that the size of the cast of any play of Shakespeare's is determined in the first instance not by the fertility of the imagination of the playwright, but by the available personnel of the company. The situation which determined the structure of plays for the smaller touring troupes of the early sixteenth century, as Bevington has shown it, had not changed fundamentally in Shakespeare's time; the companies were larger, but the determining influence was the same. Like Marlowe and Thomas Preston and Wager and Pickering before him, Shakespeare accepted the restrictions of his company. He was never free to begin with just any idea or situation which he might hope to develop; he must always begin with the actors who made up the Lord Chamberlain-King's company, for there must be roles for all of them—or nearly all of them—in every play, and he could never create any role for which there was not already a suitable actor in the company. This situation is basically different from the one which prevails in the modern theatre and which we so often assume to be universal. The dramatis personae of a new play opening in London or New York may vary from two or three characters to as many as forty or fifty for a big costume play or musical. Not so in Elizabethan England. Shakespeare never wrote a play with a cast as small as three or four, or even as small as eight or nine. Always there are fifteen or more parts, though some of the parts may be very small ones. Sometimes in the history plays as many as forty or fifty characters may appear, but the number of actors required has not been increased. The traditional dramatic practises seen in *The Marriage of Wit and Wisdom, Horestes,* and *Cambises* were still in vogue. Like his predecessors, Shakespeare has carefully arranged his large cast plays so that the members of the company may double the roles and no outsiders will be required. This practise of doubling continued as standard in his company for years after Shakespeare's retirement, even though the troupe was then larger and richer. As late as 1631 the prompt manuscript of one of the company's plays, Massinger's *Believe as You List,* shows that extensive doubling was still customary.[6]

From the modern point of view another feature of his company situation was even more restrictive for Shakespeare than the size of his troupe, a feature whose influence is to be seen in his handling of the roles of girls and women. The boys in the company were always few; even in the late and very prosperous days there were probably never more than six or seven, and there were fewer in the early days when Shakespeare was writing *Henry*

[6] Charles J. Sisson, ed., *Believe as You List By Philip Massinger, 1631.* Malone Society Reprints (Oxford, 1927).

VI and *The Two Gentlemen of Verona.* Moreover, none of the boys could have had as much experience as most of the men: the newest ones might be adequate for the roles of maids or mute court ladies, but not for much more. As a consequence of this situation in his company, the major female roles in Shakespeare's plays are few, generally only two to four large enough for the characters to have names, though there are ten to thirty named roles for the men.

In *Richard II,* for instance, there are twenty-two named parts for men, but only three for women, and none of the three is so long as the five or six leading male roles. The Queen, the Duchess of York, and the Duchess of Gloucester have 115, 89, and 58 lines respectively, and no two of them are ever on the stage at the same time; indeed, the two latter roles could easily have been played by the same boy, since the Duchess of Gloucester appears only in the first act and the Duchess of York only in the fifth.

The character and personnel of Shakespeare's company obviously led him to keep down the number and size of the female roles he prepared. No matter how poignant or charming or devious he may have found the characters of the women in the stories he was using, his first responsibility was to the fellows of his company, and the number and the state of training of the boys at most times required that not more than two or three parts for women should be given much development in the plays. So in *Henry IV*, Part 1, he could make characters of some interest and depth out of Prince Hal, Hotspur, Falstaff, King Henry, Worcester, and even Owen Glendower, but only two roles for boys could be given any scope, Lady Percy and Mistress Quickly; neither is so long as the shortest of the major men's roles, and the two characters are never on the stage at the same time.

Similarly, in his preparation of roles for the adults in his company Shakespeare needed to take care to exploit the special talents of his fellows and to shape the roles according to the abilities of the actors selected to perform them. Characters sing not simply because a song would be effective in the building of the required mood of a scene, but also because the actor for whom the role was planned was a singer. One negative aspect of this situation is rather striking. Shakespeare's genius as a song writer has frequently been commented upon; a large number of the best songs of the time are those which he wrote for his plays, and when one considers the number and the effectiveness of these songs, one tends to assume that almost any character in a Shakespearean play is likely to burst into song at one point or another. Not at all. The leading male character in a Shakespearean play almost never sings. Sometimes this lack of song in the leading role is rather surprising, as in *Romeo and Juliet,* in which the first balcony scene is a perfect situation for a serenade. Other scenes in the play also furnish situations in which a song of joy or of melancholy could very appropriately be assigned to Romeo, but Romeo never sings. And other leading characters in the plays do not sing. Hamlet does not, nor does Leontes or Prospero or Othello—to name a few for whom appropriate musical situations might easily have been devised. In other words, none of the roles which Shakespeare wrote for his principal actor, Richard Burbage, have songs written into them. There is one exception, which is particularly interesting. In the last act of *Much Ado about Nothing* Benedick *does* have four lines of a popular song, but he breaks off, and the context indicates that he sings badly. The implications are fairly clear. Shakespeare, the great song writer, wrote far more lines for Richard Burbage than he ever wrote for any other actor; most of the longest roles were prepared for him. But Burbage, the most famous actor of his time, could not sing, and consequently none of Shakespeare's scores of songs ever appears in a Burbage role.

There are other features of his acting company which influenced Shakespeare's composition of his plays, features less permanent than the limitations and the talents of the boy actors or the abilities of Richard Burbage. For a short period, for instance, the company clearly had two boy actors, one short and one tall, who were unusually good, and Shakespeare wrote for them to play together such paired roles as Helena and Hermia in *A Midsummer Night's Dream,* Portia and Nerissa in the *Merchant,* Beatrice and Hero in *Much Ado,* Rosalind and Celia in *As You Like It,* and Olivia and Viola in *Twelfth Night.* In the plays written before 1594 or after 1601 these pairs of heroines acting similar but contrasting roles together do not appear. Evidently the two boys had outgrown such parts.

Such adaptations of the plays he wrote to the requirements of the acting company with which he was associated all his life, are characteristic of the dramatist's relations with his company. Shakespeare was a great poet, as all critics have observed. But he was also a very practical man of the theatre, and this fact far fewer critics have observed; indeed many of them have tended to deny it. Shakespeare never worked in solitude, preparing ideal plays for an ideal company performing in an ideal theatre. His plays were carefully planned to make the most of the assets of a particular theatre and of the Lord Chamberlain-King's company. Ideas and interpretations which this company could not easily present in their theatre are omitted from the plays. Shakespeare's adaptation of his work to the practical requirements of his profession does not detract from his genius, as some sentimentalists seem to think. All great artists—musicians and painters, as well as poets—adapt themselves to the professional requirements in their time. Shakespeare did what Mozart did and Michelangelo did. One of the requirements of his profession in his time was that his plays should be nicely fitted to the abilities of his dramatic company. In the narrow and immediate requirements of his profession he succeeded; in the more exalted and timeless requirements of a great poetic dramatist, he also succeeded.

III.

Shakespeare and the Globe Theatre

> *Since this chapter was prepared, an excellent study of Shakespeare's plays in the environment of the Globe theatre has appeared. See Bernard Beckerman,* Shakespeare at the Globe *(New York, 1962), especially chapters 2, 3, and 5.*

JUST AS it was customary for Elizabethan playwrights to be more closely integrated with the acting companies for which they wrote than it is for modern playwrights to be, so it was normal for them to be closer to their theatres. Very few dramatists of today ever know for sure, as they write, what particular theatre their new play will be performed in; Elizabethan dramatists almost always knew. This foreknowledge characterized Elizabethan playwrights in general, for their plays were usually written to order. But for the actor-dramatists, like Thomas Heywood, and William Rowley, and Nathan Field, and William Shakespeare, the intimacy of their relation to a particular theatre was even greater than the norm. These men themselves regularly acted in the playhouses for which their own comedies and tragedies were planned. Their knowledge of what devices were invariably successful and what ones did not quite come off was based not upon an intense observation of occasional performances, but upon daily rehearsals and regular performances in which they themselves took part. Thomas Heywood knew the Red Bull theatre with the intimacy of one who worked there for years as a member of Queen Anne's company.

When one investigates a little more closely the precise ways in which individual dramatists of the reigns of Elizabeth and King James were related to their theatres, one finds again that Shakespeare's involvement with theatres was more intimate and more varied than that of any other known playwright of the time. The other principal actor-dramatists whom I have mentioned—Heywood, Rowley, and Field—were all sharers in their companies: they divided the profits; they paid the hired men; and they paid theatre rent to the housekeepers, or owners of the building. Shakespeare is the only one known who not only wrote plays for his company, acted in the plays, and shared the profits, but who was also one of the housekeepers who owned the building. For seventeen years he was one of the owners of the Globe theatre, and for eight years he was one of the housekeepers of the company's second theatre, the Blackfriars, as well. When we consider Shakespeare's planning of his plays for the theatre, therefore, we are examining his exploitation of a structure he knew not only as playwright and actor but also as part owner.

The principal London playhouses with which Shakespeare was associated during his acting and writing career were four. Early in his London life, while the theatrical situation was confused and obscure, he may have had something to do with one or two others, but the period of the late 1580's and early 1590's cannot be very clearly reconstructed now. Dramatic enterprises in these years were cursed with suppressions by the government, with long periods of quarantine because of disastrous epidemics of the plague, with bankruptcies of acting companies and consequent regroupings of actors, with long road tours necessitated by the London situation. It was not until 1594 that dramatic affairs became sufficiently settled so that one can follow the movements of the companies and their theatre tenancies with some degree of certainty.

For about three years Shakespeare and his fellows of the Lord Chamberlain's company acted at the playhouse called the Theatre, which was owned by their principal actor, Richard Burbage, his father, and his brother Cuthbert. When the Theatre was suppressed in 1597, they moved to the nearby Curtain, but a couple of years later they built their own theatre, the Globe on the Bankside. Here the company stayed for forty-three years, until long after Shakespeare's death. In 1608 they took possession of a second theatre, the private house called Blackfriars, and for thirty-four years they operated two theatres, using the Blackfriars in the winter months and the Globe during the summers. Shakespeare was thus attached to, and wrote plays for, four different playhouses, the Theatre, the Curtain, the Globe, and the Blackfriars.[1] I should point out that not all scholars agree with me that some of his last plays were written for Blackfriars. In any case, it is obvious that he pre-

[1] See E. K. Chambers, *The Elizabethan Stage* (4 vols.; Oxford, 1923), II, 199–220.

pared many more of his plays for the Globe than for any other theatre.

Shakespeare's association with the Globe, therefore, is one of the lasting influences of his life. His connection with the undertaking began before the house was built. We know about it from litigation concerning the ownership of certain shares in the Globe, a law suit in which the survivor of the Burbages told the court how their enterprise had originated many years before. Cuthbert Burbage said:

> The father of us Cuthbert and Richard Burbage was the first builder of playhouses, and was himself in his younger years a player. The Theatre he built with many hundred pounds taken up at interest ... and he had a great suit in law, and by his death the like troubles fell on us his sons. We then bethought us of altering from thence [that is from the Theatre] and at like expense built the Globe with more sums of money taken up at interest, which lay heavy on us many years, and to ourselves we joined those deserving men, Shakespeare, Heminges, Condell, Philips and other partners in the profits of that they call the House.[2]

[2] The Lord Chamberlain's Papers, Public Record Office, London. Printed in full in *Malone Society Collections*, II, Part iii (1931), 370–373. Spelling and punctuation have been modernized.

This association was a lasting one, and evidently a friendly one, for on his deathbed Shakespeare remembered these long time partners, and in his will he left

> to my fellows John Heminges, Richard Burbage, and Henry Condell 26/8 apiece to buy them rings.

The Globe, then, became the regular playhouse of the Lord Chamberlain's company of players, officially recognized. When King James came down from Scotland he issued a new patent for the company, taking them under his own patronage instead of that of the Lord Chamberlain and noting their regular theatre. The patent reads in part:

> James, by the Grace of God, &c. To all Justices, Mayors, Sheriffs, Constables, Headboroughs, and other our officers and loving subjects, greetings. Know ye that we . . . have licensed and authorized and by these presents do license and authorize these our Servants, Lawrence Fletcher, William Shakespeare, Richard Burbage, Augustine Phillipps, John Heminges, Henry Condell, William Sly, Robert Armin, Richard Cowley and the rest of their associates freely to use and exercise the Art and Faculty of playing Comedies, Tragedies, Histories, Interludes, Morals, Pastorals, Stageplays, and such others like as they have already studied

SHAKESPEARE AND THE GLOBE THEATRE

or hereafter shall use or study . . . and such like, to shew and exercise publicly to their best commodity. . . . as well within their now usual house called the Globe within our county of Surrey as also within any town halls or Moot halls or other convenient places within the liberties and freedom of any other city, university town, or borough whatsoever within our said Realms and dominions. . . .[3]

Shakespeare's association with the Globe is thus officially recognized, and it was also popularly recorded, for nine of the early quarto editions of his plays advertise the fact that they had been performed at the Globe.

Such a close and continued connection with a theatre certainly influenced the dramatist's planning of his plays, just as the character and tradition of his acting company influenced him. What can we tell of this influence?

For one thing, productions at the Globe were basically *placeless,* and Shakespeare composed all his plays with far less attention to the place of the action than modern readers assume. It is no wonder

---

[3] Patent Rolls, Public Record Office, London. Transcribed in full in *Malone Society Collections,* I, Part iii (1909), 264–265. Spelling and punctuation have been modernized.

that readers are misled, for editors of the plays have been fooling them for more than two centuries. When we read one of his plays in most modern editions we note the statement of place at the head of each scene and mentally we produce some conception of the place named as a probable setting for the scene. In *Troilus and Cressida,* for instance, our texts begin Act I, scene i with the statement "Troy. Before Priam's Palace." The second scene is headed "Troy. A Street." The third, "The Grecian Camp. Before Agamemnon's Tent." The fourth, which begins the second act, "The Grecian Camp"; the fifth "Troy. Priam's Palace" and so on through twenty-four scenes of the play, including "Pandarus' Orchard" and "Pandarus' House." It all seems very proper, since this is the sort of division and location of scenes we expect in plays. But if we look at the first edition of *Troilus and Cressida,* issued by Richard Bonian and Henry Walley in 1609, with the title page advertisement, *"As it was acted by the King's Majesty's Servants, at the Globe,"* we find that not a single one of these place designations is there. Moreover, there are no act or scene divisions at all in this first edition: it simply begins *"Enter Pandarus and Troilus,"* and it ends "FINIS," and in between there are no breaks. The second issue of the text of the play, also in 1609, is just the same. *Troilus and Cressida* was next printed in the First Folio of 1623, and again there are no divisions and no statements of place. In the folio the text does begin, *Actus Primus. Scaena Prima,* but that is the last mention of act or scene. In the second Folio of 1632, and the third of 1663, and the fourth of 1685, there are still no breaks of any kind.

To summarize, there is no edition of *Troilus and Cressida* published in the first hundred years of its existence which has any indication of place or any act and scene division. In the folios (all published after Shakespeare's death) a few plays differ from *Troilus and Cressida* in that they are divided into acts and scenes—or partially divided—but not a single play has any indication outside the dialogue of place, or change of place.

All the place statements which seem so normal to us are inventions of eighteenth-century editors, particularly Nicholas Rowe in his edition of 1709, Louis Theobald in 1733, and Sir Thomas Hanmer in 1744, and their divisions and their invented locations for each scene have been sedulously copied by nearly all editors ever since.

Why should such a careful distortion of Shakespeare's plays have been carried out and copied for centuries? The answer is ignorance. Ignorance of the theatre for which Shakespeare wrote and of his careful planning of his plays for it.

The great confusion began when Nicholas Rowe prepared the first really edited edition of Shakespeare's plays and issued it as *The Works of William Shakespeare* in six volumes in the year 1709. By this time the standard form of a London theatre had changed radically from that of the Globe. Early eighteenth-century theatres, like the Haymarket and Lincoln's Inn Fields, for which Rowe had written half a dozen plays himself, and theatres like the Drury Lane in which he most often saw Shakespeare's plays acted—these theatres were more like our twentieth-century playhouses than they were like the Globe. In the early eighteenth-century theatres, sets were commonly used, and so Nicholas Rowe invented places in which he thought the scenes of Shakespeare's plays should take place, and for early eighteenth-century readers and playgoers these suggested settings (since they conformed to the accustomed place convention) seemed not only normal, but inevitable. Unfortunately they involve a violent contradiction of the principles which governed Shakespeare and his fellow dramatists.

SHAKESPEARE AND THE GLOBE THEATRE

Shakespeare, of course, wrote with the Globe, not the Drury Lane, in mind, and he wrote a drama of persons, not a drama of places. The actor, not the setting, was paramount in a theatre like the Globe with its arrangement for intimate contact between actor and audience and its provisions for various angles of vision of the actor. Normally, in scenes written for the Globe, the audience is expected to concentrate wholly on words and actions and to ignore the place where the action may have taken place.

The first act of *Othello* is a good example of Shakespeare's customary use of his theatre, of his usual ignoring of place, with occasional emphasis on setting only when it can enhance the effect he is striving to achieve. As we read the play in modern editions, we come first to a *dramatis personae,* then a statement that the general scene is Venice and Cyprus, then a heading Act I, scene i, and then a setting, "Venice. A street." Most of this was added by Nicholas Rowe; it did not appear in the first quarto. Shakespeare planned his play to begin simply with the conversation of Iago and Roderigo, with no one in the audience concerning himself with the setting for their conversation. At line 74 the setting does have some significance, and with

Iago's remark, "Here is her father's house" the permanent stage facade becomes Brabantio's house front and so remains until the end of the scene.

At the beginning of the next scene (when Othello, Iago, and servants enter) the stage is placeless again. For 47 lines there is no indication of setting at all. Then Othello says to Iago and Cassio:

> 'Tis well I am found by you.
> I will but spend a word here in the house,
> And go with you.

He goes in, and Cassio says to Iago,

> Ancient, what makes he *here?*

The scene thus changes at lines 48 and 49 from an indefinite place to a particular place, and the stage facade, which a short time before was Brabantio's house, is now the front of the house in which Othello is staying with Desdemona. It continues so for the remaining fifty lines of the scene. Toward the end of this second scene of the act, Shakespeare begins to prepare the Globe audience for the localization of the action which is to follow, for the last scene of the act is to be one in which place *is* important, as it had not been in the previous two. This preparation begins at line 92, when the Officer says to Brabantio,

> 'Tis true, most worthy signior.
> The Duke's in council, and your noble self
> I am sure is sent for.

And Brabantio replies:

> How? The Duke in council?
> In this time of night? Bring him away!
> Mine's not an idle cause. The Duke himself,
> Or any of my brothers of the state,
> Cannot but feel this wrong as 'twere their own.

The following scene, the third in Act I, is to be the emergency night meeting of the Duke and the Senators in the Venetian Council Chamber. These lines of the Officers and Brabantio prepare for it, and the opening stage direction, as printed in the first quarto, shows how the scene was planned to be localized at the Globe:

> *Enter Duke and Senators, set at a Table with lights and Attendants.*

In this scene, unlike the first two, the environment of the action is of some importance. The tone of national emergency is developed as the Duke and Senators compare their fateful (but contradictory) dispatches, and the messengers hurry in and out. For forty-six lines the attention of the audience is held to the crisis in the affairs of the state of Venice and focused on the authority of this august body which is considering momentous affairs around the council table. It is important for the audience at the Globe to be conscious of the place in this scene. In such an environment of high decision and national crisis, surely the petty affair of the runaway daughter of a Venetian senator will be brushed aside as insignificant. When precisely the opposite proves to be the case, and the Duke and the Council of the Senators of Venice suspend their vital deliberations for one hundred and eighty lines to hear the case of Desdemona and Othello, the importance of Othello is dramatically established in the eyes of the audience. The localization of this third scene in the first act is thus used, not in our modern way as a standard convention for all scenes, but in order to achieve a particular effect important for the production of *Othello* at the Globe.

Another example of Shakespeare's use of the normally placeless character of his stage is to be seen in his favorite method of presenting military action. Often such battle scenes are the climactic meeting of the opposing forces in the play; many times he dramatized episodes in a battle as part of a panoramic view of the whole conflict and the characteristic parts in this conflict played by the major characters. In such situations the placeless character of the Globe stage was very useful; it enabled Shakespeare to fuse together his episodes without distracting the audience by localities for each scene.

A fairly characteristic example is the fifth act of *Julius Caesar*. Here all the principal characters of the play are concentrated at the Battle of Philippi; one set of characters after another is brought forward during the battle and the preparations for it. The action is continuous but episodic, and the location of any particular episode is irrelevant. This flowing, uninterrupted action could be made effective on the Globe stage. But when the placeless character of the stage for which *Julius Caesar* had been written was forgotten, the editors had trouble with this act. Several eighteenth-century editors divided it up into nine different scenes, which could be justified for a Drury Lane production, but which make Shakespeare's flowing panoramic action appear to be jumpy and inconclusive.

Twentieth-century editors generally reduce these nine scenes to five, which is some improvement, but which still throws the action out of focus because the setting of each scene is carefully emphasized, generally called "Another part of the field." The point is that the audience is not supposed to think of place at all, but to concentrate on the decision of Brutus, the confusion of Cassius, and the finality of the battle.

In other of Shakespeare's plays this basically placeless character of his stage is exploited for effects which can easily be missed in modern texts with excessive divisions, and they are often missed in productions. One of the dramatic devices constantly employed by Shakespeare and by his fellow dramatists is scene contrast; that is, the dramatic impact of a particular scene is greatly enhanced by the sharply contrasted tone or content of the scene which preceded it. Such effects depend upon continuous performance; any break or interruption between such paired scenes spoils, or greatly reduces, the effect. On Shakespeare's stage there was no intermission between scenes at all, so that one scene flowed into another with no interruption of the concentration of the audience. Such continuity is greatly facilitated by the placeless stage where—in most instances—no pause for removal or addition of properties is required. Often in modern editions the designation of a new place and the strongly marked scene break spoil the effect.

Such exploitation of the placeless character of his stage is a regular practice with Shakespeare. Other customary planning for the assets of the Globe, its provisions for asides and soliloquies, for elevated scenes, for the immediate impact of episodes of contrasted tone, and for simultaneous entrances, are apparent in all the plays of the middle period.

The features of the Globe, with which he was associated as actor, playwright, sharer, and housekeeper are important for his plays. Without some knowledge of these standard Elizabethan stage practices it is fatally easy to misunderstand situations, to mutilate delicate effects, to see defects which are not there and to remedy them by highhanded and misguided textual emendations. Since William Shakespeare was so clearly a man of the theatre, it can be disastrous to try to understand the man while ignoring the theatre.

IV.

Shakespeare and the Blackfriars Theatre

I am grateful to the Cambridge University Press for permission to reprint this piece in a modified form.

IN THE preceding chapters I have contended that the popular tendency to concentrate on Shakespeare the poet, preparing his plays with constant consideration for the reader in the study, is misguided, an implied contradiction of all that we have been able to discover about the life of the man and the texts of his plays. The facts of biography and bibliography which have been assembled by hundreds of scholars in the last two centuries consistently suggest that the environment in which this man worked was not that of the study but of the professional theatre and the professional acting company. Some of the general characteristics of this theatre and of the acting troupe and the general influence they exercised over Shakespeare have been outlined in the second and third chapters.

More specific influences on the career and the plays of Shakespeare are surely to be found if we look at the plays in their proper environment. Since Shakespeare was more completely and more continuously involved with theatres and acting companies than any other Elizabethan dramatist whose life we know, some consideration of such particular influences of these professional associations ought to be suggestive. In his long and absorbing association with the Lord Chamberlain-King's company and their theatres there are a number of events which one would expect to have influenced his work. One of the earliest must have been the protracted plague closing of all theatres in 1593 and 1594, for out of this disaster to all London players the Lord Chamberlain's company apparently rose. Another must have been the assembling of the players and the drawing up of the agreement for the formal organization of the Lord Chamberlain's company. The record suggests that Shakespeare was one of the leaders in this organization, for when the new company performed before the court in the Christmas season of 1594–1595, payment was made to Richard Burbage, the principal actor, Will Kemp, the principal comedian, and William Shakespeare.[1] How did the great possibilities offered by this new troupe, destined to become the most famous and most successful in the history of the English theatre, initially affect the writing of its chief dramatist?

In the winter of 1598–1599 occurred another event which must have been of absorbing interest for all members of the company. This was, of course, the building of the Globe on the Bankside. Here was a theatre built for the occupancy of a particular company, and six of the seven owners were actors in the company. Assuredly it was built, so far as available funds would allow, to the specific requirements of the productions of the Lord Chamberlain's men. What facilities did Shakespeare get which he had not had before? How did he alter his composition to take advantage of the new possibilities? Can there be any doubt that as a successful man of the theatre he did so?

The next event which must have been of great importance for Shakespeare and his troupe was their involvement in the Essex rebellion. This exceptional case has received the full attention of

[1] "Dramatic Records in the Declared Accounts of the Treasurer of the Chamber, 1558–1642," *Malone Society Collections,* VI (1962), 29.

critics and scholars because of its supposed relation to a performance of Shakespeare's *Richard II*. Actually, however, the Essex rebellion, much though it must have excited the company for a few months, was the least influential of all these factors affecting the company's activities and Shakespeare's development. Apparently the company's innocence was established without much difficulty. There is no clear indication that their later performances or Shakespeare's later writing were affected by the experience. Though the events were sensational, and though they must have caused great anxiety for a time, they cannot be thought of as events of long-term significance in the history of this group of men who were so influential in Shakespeare's career and development.

Of much more importance in the affairs of the company was their attainment of the patronage of James I less than two months after the death of Elizabeth. This patronage and the King's livery certainly became one of the important factors in creating the great prestige of the company. In the ten years before they became the King's company, their known performances at court average about three a year; in the ten years after they attained their new service their known performances at court average about thirteen a year, more than those of all other London companies combined.[2] They were officially the premier company in London; a good part of their time must have been devoted to the preparation of command performances. Surely this new status of the troupe must have been a steady and pervasive influence in the development of its principal dramatist, William Shakespeare.

The final event which I wish to mention in the affairs of the King's company was perhaps the most important of all. There is no doubt that it made a great change in the activities of the company, and I do not see how it can have failed to be an influence in Shakespeare's development as a dramatist. This event was the acquisition of the famous private theatre in Blackfriars. No adult company in London had ever before performed regularly in a private theatre. For thirty years the private theatres with their superior audiences, their concerts, their comfortable accommodations, their traffic in sophisticated drama and the latest literary fads, had been the exclusive homes of the boy companies, the pets

[2] E. K. Chambers, *The Elizabethan Stage* (4 vols.; Oxford, 1923), IV, 108–130.

of Society.[3] Now for the first time a troupe of those rogues and vagabonds, the common players, had the temerity to present themselves to the sophisticates of London in a repertory at the town's most exclusive theatre. I shall suggest later that this was one of the turning points in Tudor and Stuart dramatic history. Beaumont and Jonson and Fletcher had begun to make the craft of the playwright more socially respectable. The increasing patronage of the drama by the royal family, and the growing splendour and frequency of the court masques which were written by ordinary playwrights and performed in part by common players, were raising the prestige of the drama and the theatre from its Elizabethan to its Caroline state. The acquisition of the Blackfriars in 1608 by the King's company and the full exploitation of the new playhouse must have been the most conspicuous evidence to Londoners of the changing state of affairs. Surely it is impossible that the King's men and their principal dramatist, William Shakespeare, could have been

[3] The differences between the two types of theatres and companies have been extensively discussed by Alfred Harbage in *Shakespeare and the Rival Traditions* (New York, 1952). Some of his categorizing of plays, playwrights, and moral attitudes seems to me to be too rigid, but his general analysis of the two types of theatre is sound.

unaware of this situation. Surely they must have bent all their efforts in the selection and performance of old plays and in the commissioning and writing of new ones to the full exploitation of this unprecedented opportunity. The new state of affairs must have been apparent in much that they did, and it must have influenced the dramatic compositions of Shakespeare.

So far, it has been my contention that all we know of William Shakespeare has shown him to be above all else a man of the theatre, that during the twenty years of his creative maturity most of his time was spent in closest association with members of the Lord Chamberlain-King's company and in thought about their needs and their interests, and that therefore in the affairs of this company we should seek one of the principal influences in his creative life. I have mentioned six events which (so far as we can tell through the mists of three hundred and fifty years) seem to have been important in the affairs of that theatrical organization. These events are not all of equal importance, but each of them, except possibly the Essex rebellion, must have had a marked effect on the activities of Shakespeare's company and therefore on the dramatic creations of Shakespeare himself. Each one, it seems to me, deserves more study than it has received in its relation to the development of Shakespeare's work.

Let me invite attention now to a fuller consideration of one of the most important of these events in the history of the Lord Chamberlain-King's company, namely the acquisition of the Blackfriars theatre. What did this event mean in the history of the company, and how did it affect the writing of William Shakespeare?

Probably we should note first the time at which the Blackfriars would have begun to influence the company and the writing of Shakespeare. All the dramatic histories say that the King's men took over the Blackfriars theatre in 1608, and this is true in a legal sense, for on 9 August 1608 leases were executed conveying the Blackfriars Playhouse to seven lessees: Cuthbert Burbage, Thomas Evans, and five members of the King's company—John Heminges, William Sly, Henry Condell, Richard Burbage, and William Shakespeare. The few scholars who have examined in detail the history of the King's company have noted, however, that Shakespeare and his fellows probably did not begin to act at the Blackfriars in August of 1608. The plague was rife in London at that time; fifty plague deaths had been recorded for the week ending 28 July, and for a year and a half, or until December 1609, the bills of mortality show an abnormally high death rate from the plague. Though specific records about the closing of the theatres are not extant, we have definite statements that they were closed for part of this period, and comparison with other years suggests that there must have been very little if any public acting allowed in London between the first of August 1608 and the middle of December 1609. Therefore, it has occasionally been said, the Blackfriars was not used by the King's men much before 1610, and no influence on their plays and their productions can be sought before that year.

This conclusion of little or no influence before 1610 is, I think, a false one. It is based on the erroneous assumption that the actors and playwrights of the King's company would have known nothing about the peculiarities of the Blackfriars and that they would have had no plays prepared especially for that theatre until after they had begun performing in it. Actors are never so stupid or so insular as this in any time. The King's men, we may be sure, were well aware of the Blackfriars and the type of performance it required, or specialized in, long before they came to lease the theatre. There must be many evidences of this, but three in particular come readily to mind.

Seven years before, in 1601, the King's men had been involved in the War of the Theatres, which was in part a row between the public theatres and the private theatres. The chief attack on the public theatres and adult actors was made in Jonson's *Poetaster,* performed at the Blackfriars. Certain actors of the Lord Chamberlain's company, and possibly Shakespeare himself, were ridiculed in this Blackfriars play. The reply, *Satiromastix,* was written by Thomas Dekker and performed by Shakespeare's company at the Globe.[4] Certainly in 1601 at least, the company was well aware of the goings on at Blackfriars.

A second piece of evidence pointing to their knowledge of the peculiar requirements of the Blackfriars is the case of Marston's *Malcontent.* Marston wrote this play for the boys at the Blackfriars, who performed it in that theatre in 1604. The King's men stole the play, as they admitted, and performed it at the Globe; the third edition,

---

[4] See J. H. Penniman, *The War of the Theatres* (Boston, 1897), and R. A. Small, *The Stage Quarrel* (Breslau, 1899).

also 1604, shows the alterations they commissioned John Webster to make in order to adapt a Blackfriars script to a Globe performance, and in the induction to the play Richard Burbage, speaking in his own person, points out one or two of the differences between Blackfriars requirements and Globe requirements.

Finally, and most familiar of all evidence that the King's men were quite alive to what went on at Blackfriars, is the "little eyases" passage in *Hamlet* and Shakespeare's rueful admission that, for a time at any rate, the competition of the Blackfriars was too much for the company at the Globe.

Clearly the King's men did not have to wait until their performances of 1610 at the Blackfriars to know how their plays needed to be changed to fit them to that theatre and its select audience. They had known for several years what the general characteristics of Blackfriars performances were. Indeed, the leading member of the company, Richard Burbage, had a double reason for being familiar with all the peculiarities of the Blackfriars, for since his father's death in 1597 he had been the owner of the theatre and the landlord of the boy company that made it famous. We can be perfectly sure, then, that from the day of the first proposal that the King's men take over the Blackfriars they had talked among themselves about what they would do with it and had discussed what kinds of plays they would have to have written to exploit it. It is all too often forgotten that in all such discussions among the members of the King's company William Shakespeare would have had an important part. He had more kinds of connections with the company than any other man: he was actor, shareholder, patented member, principal playwright, and one of the housekeepers of the Globe; even Burbage did not serve so many functions in the company.

When would the King's men have begun planning for their performances at the Blackfriars? We cannot, of course, set the exact date, but we can approximate it. There is one faint suggestion that consideration of the project may have started very early indeed. Richard Burbage said that Henry Evans, who had leased the Blackfriars from him for the Children of the Queen's Revels, began talking to him about the surrender of his lease in 1603 or 1604.[5] These early discussions evidently came to

---

[5] The Answers of Heminges and Burbage to Edward Kirkham, 1612, printed by F. G. Fleay, *A Chronicle History of the London Stage* (London, 1890), p. 235.

nothing, for we know that the boys continued in the theatre for three or four years longer. Burbage's statement about Evans does suggest the interesting possibility that the King's men may have dallied with the project of leasing the Blackfriars theatre as early as 1603 or 1604. This, however, is only the faintest of possibilities. The Blackfriars was tentatively in the market then, but all we know is that Burbage had to consider for a short time the possibility of getting other tenants for his theatre. Whether the King's men came to his mind and theirs as possible tenants, we do not know.

We can be sure that active planning for performances at the Blackfriars did get under way when Burbage, who was both the leading actor of the King's men and owner of the Blackfriars theatre, knew for certain that the boy actors would give up their lease and that arrangements for a syndicate of King's men to take over the theatre could be made. Conferences among these men—the Burbages, Heminges, Condell, Shakespeare, and Sly—and probably preliminary financial arrangements would have been going on before a scrivener was called in to draw up a rough draft of the lease. Such preliminaries, which must come before a lease can be formally signed, often consume months. We know that the leases were formally executed on 9 August 1608; therefore discussions in June and July or even in April and May are likely enough. We know that the Blackfriars theatre was available as early as March 1608, for in a letter dated 11 March 1608 Sir Thomas Lake officially notified Lord Salisbury that the company of the Children of Blackfriars must be suppressed and that the King had vowed that they should never act again even if they had to beg their bread. General confirmation of this fact is found in a letter written two weeks later by the French ambassador.[6] It is evident that in March of 1608 Richard Burbage knew his theatre was without a tenant; March to July 1608, then, are the months for discussions among the King's men of prospective performances at the Blackfriars.

What did this little group of Shakespeare and his intimate associates of the last fourteen years work out during their discussions in the months of March to July 1608? One of the things they must have considered was alterations of their style of acting. As Granville-Barker has pointed out,[7] the acting in the new Blackfriars before a sophisticated

[6] *The Elizabethan Stage*, II, 53–54.
[7] *Prefaces to Shakespeare* (2 vols.; Princeton, 1946), I, 470–471.

audience would have to be more quiet than in the large open-air Globe before the groundlings. It would be easier to emphasize points in the quiet candlelit surroundings, and "sentiment will become as telling as passion." There must also have been extended discussions of what to do about the repertory: which of the company's plays would be suitable for the elegant new theatre and which should be kept for the old audience at the Globe? Some of their decisions are fairly obvious. *Mucedorus*, which Rafe in *The Knight of the Burning Pestle* says he had played before the Wardens of his company and which went through fifteen editions before the Restoration, was clearly one of the Globe plays which might be laughed at by a Blackfriars audience. Similarly, *The Merry Devil of Edmonton* was not a good Blackfriars prospect. Certain other plays in the repertory might be expected to please at the Blackfriars; Marston's *Malcontent*, for instance, could easily be changed back to its original Blackfriars form, and Jonson's *Every Man in His Humour* and *Every Man out of His Humour*, though nine and ten years old, had been played by the company at court in the last three years and ought to be suitable for the Blackfriars.

These discussions of the old repertory, though no

doubt important to the company then, are fruitless for us now. I know of no evidence as to their decisions. More important are the proposals for new plays for the Blackfriars, and I think we do have some evidence as to what these decisions were. The experienced members of the King's company were familiar with the fact so commonly recorded in the annals of the Jacobean theatre that new plays were in constant demand. With the acquisition of the new theatre they had an opportunity to claim for their own the most profitable audience in London. We know from the later Jacobean and Caroline records that this is just what they did. It seems likely that one of the foundations of their later unquestioned dominance of the audiences of the gentry was their decision about plays and playwrights made in their discussions of March to July 1608.

One of their decisions, I suggest, was to get Jonson to write Blackfriars plays for them. He was a likely choice for three reasons. First, because he was developing a following among the courtly audience (always prominent at the Blackfriars) by his great court masques. At this time he had already written his six early entertainments for King James —those at the Coronation, at the Opening of Parliament, at Althorp, at Highgate, and the two at Theobalds. He had written for performance at Whitehall *The Masque of Blackness, The Masque of Beauty, Hymenaei,* and *Lord Haddington's Masque.* The sensational success of these courtly entertainments made Jonson a most promising choice to write plays for the courtly audience which the King's men did succeed in attracting to Blackfriars.

A second reason which would have led the King's men to Jonson as a writer for their new theatre was his great reputation among the literati and critics. In this decade from 1601 to 1610 the literary allusions to him are numerous, more numerous than to Shakespeare himself. The poems to Jonson and the long prose passages about him in this time are far more frequent than to Shakespeare; quotations from his work occur oftener, and I find three times as many literary and social references to performances of his plays and masques as to Shakespeare's. Poems about him or references to his work are written in these years by John Donne, Sir John Roe, Sir Dudley Carleton, the Venetian ambassador, John Chamberlain, Sir Thomas Lake, Sir George Buc, Sir Thomas Salusbury.[8] These men represent just the kind of audience which might be attracted to the Blackfriars, and which, eventually, the King's men did attract there.

There was a third reason which would have made Jonson seem to the King's men a very likely bet for their new theatre: he had already had experience in writing plays for this theatre when it was occupied by boys. Before the conferences of the King's men about their new project he had already had performed at Blackfriars *Cynthia's Revels, The Poetaster, The Case Is Altered,* and *Eastward Ho.* Possibly just before the time of the conferences of the King's men he had been writing for the Blackfriars another play, *Epicoene,* for he says in the Folio of 1616 that the play was performed by the Children of Blackfriars, but the date he gives for performance comes after their expulsion from the Blackfriars theatre. Not only had Jonson had the valuable experience of writing four or five plays for the Blackfriars, but the Induction to *Cynthia's Revels* and his personal statements about boys of

[8] See G. E. Bentley, *Shakespeare and Jonson* (2 vols.; Chicago, 1945), I, 38–41, 65–67, 73–79, 87–90; II, 15–22; and Bradley and Adams, *The Jonson Allusion-Book* (New Haven, 1922), pp. 9–78.

the company, like Nathan Field and Solomon Pavy suggest that he had directed them in their rehearsals. What valuable experience for the King's men planning their first performance in this new theatre!

Now all these qualifications of Jonson as a prospect for the King's men are, in sober fact, only speculations. Perhaps they simply show that if *I* had been participating in the conferences about the Blackfriars I should have argued long and lustily for Ben Jonson. Alas, I was not there! What evidence is there that they really did agree to secure his services for the company? The evidence is that *before* these conferences he had written only four plays for the Lord Chamberlain's or King's company—three, nine, and ten years before—nothing for the company in the years 1605–1608. *After* these conferences, he wrote all his remaining plays for the company, with the exception of *Bartholomew Fair* six years later, a play which he gave to his good friend and protégé Nathan Field for the Lady Elizabeth's company at the Hope, and *A Tale of a Tub,* twenty-five years later, which he gave to Queen Henrietta's men. Jonson's first play after the reopening of Blackfriars was *The Alchemist*; it was written for the King's men, and numerous allusions show clearly that it was written for Blackfriars. So were *Catiline, The Devil Is an Ass, The Staple of News, The New Inn,* and *The Magnetic Lady.* Of course we lack the final proof of recorded reference to a definite agreement, but the evidence is such as to suggest that one of the decisions reached by the King's men in the reorganization of their enterprise to exploit the great advantages of their new theatre was to secure the services of Ben Jonson to write plays for the literate and courtly audience at Blackfriars.

Another decision, which I suggest the King's men made at these conferences, was to secure for their new theatre the services of the rising young collaborators, Francis Beaumont and John Fletcher. These gentlemen were younger than Jonson by about ten years, and as yet their reputations were distinctly inferior to his, but they had already displayed those talents which were to make their plays the stage favorites at Blackfriars for the next thirty-four years, and were to cause Dryden to say sixty years later that "their plays are now the most pleasant and frequent entertainments of the stage."

One of the great assets of Beaumont and Fletcher was social. In the years immediately before and after 1608 the London audience was developing the social cleavage which is such a marked characteristic of the Caroline drama and stage. In Elizabeth's time the London public theatre audience was a universal one. The later Jacobean and the Caroline audience was a dual one: the gentry, the court, the professional classes, and the Inns of Court went to the Blackfriars, the Phoenix, and later to the Salisbury Court; the London masses went to the larger and noisier Red Bull and Fortune and Globe. This situation will be set forth more fully in the next chapter.

This new state of affairs was just developing when the King's men had their conferences about the Blackfriars in 1608. They evidently saw what was coming, however, for in the next few years they understood and exploited the situation more effectively than any other troupe in London. Indeed, the very acquisition of the Blackfriars and its operation in conjunction with the Globe was a device which had never been tried before in London and which is the clearest evidence that the King's men knew what was happening.

Under these circumstances, then, the social status of Beaumont and Fletcher was an asset for the company in their new house. Francis Beaumont came of an ancient and distinguished Leicestershire family, with many connections among the nobility. John Fletcher was the son of a Lord Bishop of London and one-time favourite of Elizabeth. To a Blackfriars audience the social standing of these two young men would have been more acceptable than that of any other dramatist writing in London in 1608.

Another asset which made Beaumont and Fletcher valuable for the new enterprise of the King's men was their private theatre experience. So far as we can make out now, all their plays before this time had been written for private theatres and most of them for the Blackfriars. *The Woman Hater* had been prepared for the private theatre in St. Paul's, but *The Knight of the Burning Pestle*, *The Scornful Lady,* and *The Faithful Shepherdess* were Blackfriars plays. I think we can add to this list *Cupid's Revenge*. This play has been variously dated, but two articles by James Savage[9] seem to me to offer convincing evidence that the play was prepared for Blackfriars about 1607 and that it displays a crude preliminary working out of much of

---

[9] "The Date of Beaumont and Fletcher's *Cupid's Revenge*" and "Beaumont and Fletcher's *Philaster* and Sidney's *Arcadia,*" *ELH,* XV (1948), 286–294 and XIV (1947), 194–206.

the material which made *Philaster* one of the great hits of its time and one of the more influential plays of the seventeenth century. In any event, Beaumont and Fletcher were among the most experienced Blackfriars playwrights available in 1608. It is true that in 1608 none of their plays had been a great success; indeed the two best, *The Knight of the Burning Pestle* and *The Faithful Shepherdess,* are known to have been unsuccessful at first. The King's men, however, were experienced in the ways of the theatre; it does not seem rash to assume that at least one of them knew enough about audiences and about dramatic talents to see that these young men were writers of brilliant theatrical promise—especially since that one was William Shakespeare.

Beaumont and Fletcher, then, because of their experience and social standing were very desirable dramatists for the King's men to acquire in 1608 for their new private theatre. What is the evidence that they did acquire them? The evidence is that all the Beaumont and Fletcher plays of the next few years are King's men's plays, several of them famous hits—*Philaster, The Maid's Tragedy, A King and No King, The Captain, The Two Noble Kinsmen, Bonduca, Monsieur Thomas, Valentinian.* The dating of many of the Beaumont and

Fletcher plays is very uncertain because of their late publication, and it may be that two or three of the later plays were written for other companies, but at least forty-five plays by Beaumont and Fletcher were the property of the Jacobean and Caroline King's men.[10] None of their plays before 1608, when Blackfriars was acquired, was, so far as we can find, written for the King's men. It seems a reasonable conclusion, therefore, that another of the policies agreed upon at the conferences of 1608 was to secure the services of Beaumont and Fletcher for the company in its new enterprise at the Blackfriars.

The third of these three important changes in policy which I think the King's men agreed upon at their conferences about the new Blackfriars enterprise, is the most interesting of all to us, but it was the easiest and most obvious for them. Indeed, it may well have been assumed almost without discussion. It was, of course, that William Shakespeare should write henceforth with the Blackfriars in mind and not the Globe.

Why was this decision an easy and obvious one? The company could assume, of course, that he

[10] G. E. Bentley, *The Jacobean and Caroline Stage* (5 vols.; Oxford, 1941–1956), I, 109–115.

would continue to write for them, because he was a shareholder and a patented member of the company and a housekeeper in both their theatres. Since the formation of the company, fourteen years before, all his plays had been written for performance by them, always, in the last nine years, for performance at the Globe. All his professional associations as well as his financial ones were with this company, and probably no one in the group even considered his defection. Burbage, Shakespeare, Heminges, and Condell were the real nucleus of the organization.

This new enterprise at the Blackfriars was a very risky business. As we have noted, no adult company had ever tried to run a private theatre before. The King's men not only proposed to make a heavy investment in this new departure, but they intended to continue running their old public theatre at the same time. Every possible precaution against failure needed to be taken. One such precaution would be the devotion of Shakespeare's full-time energies to the Blackfriars instead of the Globe. They could trust Shakespeare; he knew their potentialities and their shortcomings as no other dramatist did—indeed, few dramatists in the history of the English theatre have ever had such a long and intimate association with an acting company as William Shakespeare had with these men. If anybody knew what Burbage and Heminges and Condell and Robert Armyn and Richard Cowley could do on the stage and what they should not be asked to do, that man was William Shakespeare. He could make them a success at the Blackfriars as they had been at the Globe if any one could.

Another reason for the transfer of Shakespeare's efforts was the fact that the Globe could be left largely to take care of itself with an old repertory as the Blackfriars could not. For one thing, there was no old repertory for the Blackfriars, since the departing boys appear to have held on to their old plays. For another thing, it was the Blackfriars audience which showed the greater avidity for new plays; the public theatre audiences were much more faithful to old favourites. They were still watching *Friar Bacon and Friar Bungay* at the Fortune in 1630 and Marlowe's *Edward II* at the Red Bull in 1620 and *Dr. Faustus* at the Fortune in 1621 and *Richard II* and *Pericles* at the Globe in 1631. In the archives of the Globe at this time there must have been a repertory of more than a hundred plays, including at least twenty-five of Shakespeare's. Moreover, certain plays written for the Globe in the last few years, like Wilkins's *Miseries of Enforced Marriage* and the anonymous *Yorkshire Tragedy* and *The Fair Maid of Bristol* and *The London Prodigal*, had provided playwrights who might be expected to entertain a Globe audience with more of the same fare, but who could scarcely come up to the requirements of sophistication at Blackfriars. Altogether, then, the Globe repertory had much less need of Shakespeare's efforts in 1608 than did the Blackfriars repertory.

Why should Shakespeare have wanted to write for the Blackfriars, or at least have agreed to do so? The most elementary of the apparent reasons is that he had money invested in the project and stood to lose by its failure and gain by its success. He was one of the seven lessees of the new theatre; he had paid down an unknown sum and had agreed to pay £5 14s.4d. per year in rent.[11] He had at least a financial reason for doing everything he could to establish the success of the Blackfriars venture, and what Shakespeare could do most effectively was to write plays which would insure the company's popularity with the audience in its new private theatre.

[11] E. K. Chambers, *William Shakespeare* (2 vols.; Oxford, 1930), II, 62–63.

A third reason for this postulated decision of the King's men in 1608 to have Shakespeare devote his entire attention to the Blackfriars and abandon the Globe was that the King's men saw that the real future of theatrical prosperity in London lay with the court and the court party in the private theatres. Their receipts for performances at court showed them this very clearly. In the last nine years of Elizabeth, 1594–1602, they had received from court performances an average of £35 a year; in the first five years of the reign of the new king, 1603–1607, they had averaged £131 per year in addition to their new allowances for liveries as servants of the King.[12] The Blackfriars and not the Globe was the theatre where they could entertain this courtly audience with commercial performances. There is no doubt that in the next few years after 1608 the Blackfriars did become the principal theatre of the company. In 1612 Edward Kirkham said they took £1,000 a winter more at the Blackfriars than they had formerly taken at the Globe.[13] When Sir Henry Herbert listed receipts from the two theatres early in the reign of King Charles, the

[12] *The Elizabethan Stage*, IV, 164–175.
[13] C. W. Wallace, *University of Nebraska Studies*, VIII (1908), 36–37, n. 6.

receipts for single performances at the Globe averaged £6 13s.8d.; those for single performances at the Blackfriars averaged £15 15s., or about two and one-half times as much.[14] In 1634 an Oxford don who wrote up the company simply called them the company of the Blackfriars and did not mention the Globe at all;[15] when the plays of the company were published in the Jacobean and Caroline period, the Blackfriars was mentioned as their theatre more than four times as often as the Globe was.[16] Such evidence proves that the Blackfriars certainly did become the principal theatre of the King's men. I am suggesting that in the conferences of 1608 the King's men had some intimation that it would, and accordingly they persuaded William Shakespeare to devote his attention to that theatre in the future instead of to the Globe.

So much for the reasons that Shakespeare might be *expected* to change the planning of his plays in 1608. What is the evidence that he did? The evidence, it seems to me, is to be seen in *Cymbeline, The Winter's Tale, The Tempest,* and *The Two Noble Kinsmen,* and probably it was to be seen

[14] *The Jacobean and Caroline Stage,* I, 23–24.
[15] *Ibid.,* p. 26, n. 5.
[16] *Ibid.,* p. 30, n. 1.

also in the lost play, *Cardenio.* The variations which these plays show from the Shakespearean norm have long been a subject for critical comment. The first three of them in particular, since they are the only ones which have been universally accepted as part of the Shakespeare canon, have commonly been discussed as a distinct genre. Widely as critics and scholars have disagreed over the reasons for their peculiar characteristics, those peculiarities have generally been recognized, whether the plays are called Shakespeare's Romances, or Shakespeare's Tragi-Comedies, or his Romantic Tragi-Comedies, or simply the plays of the fourth period. Few competent critics who have read carefully through the Shakespeare canon have failed to recognize that there is something different about *Cymbeline, The Winter's Tale, The Tempest,* and *The Two Noble Kinsmen.*

When critics and scholars have tried to explain this difference between the plays of the last period and Shakespeare's earlier work, they have set up a variety of hypotheses. Most of these hypotheses agree only in considering Shakespeare as the professional poet and not the professional playwright. They turn to Shakespeare's sources, or to his inspiration, or to his personal affairs, or to the bucolic environment of his Stratford retirement, or to his philosophic development, but not to the theatre which was his daily preoccupation for more than twenty years. Dowden called this late group in the Shakespeare canon "On the Heights," because he thought the plays reflected Shakespeare's newfound serenity. Such fine optimism had, perhaps, something to recommend it to the imaginations of the Victorians, but to most modern scholars it seems to throw more light on Dowden's mind than on Shakespeare's development. Dowden's explanation seemed utterly fatuous to Lytton Strachey, who thought that the plays of "Shakespeare's Final Period" were written by a Shakespeare far from serene, who was really "half enchanted by visions of beauty and loveliness and half bored to death." Traversi calls the plays Shakespeare's "last symbolic comedies."[17] Violently as Dowden and Strachey and Traversi differ, they agree in seeking subjective interpretations.

One of the best known of the old explanations of

[17] Edward Dowden, "Shakspere's Last Plays," *Shakspere: A Critical Study of His Mind and Art* (3rd ed.; New York, 1902). Lytton Strachey, "Shakespeare's Final Period," *Books and Characters: French and English* (New York, 1922). Derek Traversi, *Shakespeare: The Last Phase* (New York, [1954]).

the peculiarities of the plays of this last period is Thorndike's:[18] the contention that the great success of *Philaster* caused Shakespeare to imitate it in *Cymbeline* and to a lesser extent in *The Winter's Tale* and *The Tempest*. In spite of the great horror of the Shakespeare idolaters at the thought of the master imitating superficial young whipper-snappers like Beaumont and Fletcher, few can read the two plays together without noting the similarities between them. The difficulty is that although the approximate dates of the two plays are clear enough, their *precise* dates are so close together and so uncertain that neither Thorndike nor any subsequent scholar has been able to prove that *Philaster* came before *Cymbeline,* and the Shakespeare idolaters have been equally unable to prove that *Cymbeline* came before *Philaster*.

I suggest that the really important point is not the priority of either play. The significant and revealing facts are that both were written for the King's company; both were written, or at least completed, after the important decision made by the leaders of the troupe in the spring of 1608 to commission new plays for Blackfriars, and both were

[18] Ashley H. Thorndike, *The Influence of Beaumont and Fletcher on Shakespeare* (Worcester, Mass., 1901).

prepared to be acted in the private theatre in Blackfriars before the sophisticated audience attracted to that house. It is their common purpose and environment, not imitation of one by the other, which makes them similar. Both *Philaster* and *Cymbeline* are somewhat like Beaumont and Fletcher's earlier plays, especially *Cupid's Revenge,* because Beaumont and Fletcher's earlier plays had all been written for private theatres and all but one for Blackfriars. Both *Philaster* and *Cymbeline* are unlike Shakespeare's earlier plays because none of those plays had been written for private theatres. The subsequent plays of both Beaumont and Fletcher and Shakespeare have certain resemblances to *Philaster* and *Cymbeline* because they too were written to be performed by the King's men before the sophisticated and courtly audience in the private theatre at Blackfriars.

So much I think we can say with some assurance. This explanation of the character of Shakespeare's last plays is in accord with the known facts of theatrical history; it accords with the biographical evidence of Shakespeare's long and close association with all the enterprises of the Lord Chamberlain–King's men for twenty years; it is in accord with his fabulously acute sense of the theatre and the problems of the actor; and it does no violence to his artistic integrity or to his poetic genius.

May I add one further point much more in the realm of speculation? Since John Fletcher became a playwright for the King's men at this time and continued so for the remaining seventeen years of his life, and since the activities of the King's men had been one of Shakespeare's chief preoccupations for many years, is it not likely that the association between Fletcher and Shakespeare from 1608 to 1614 was closer than has usually been thought? Shakespeare was nearing retirement; after 1608 he wrote plays less frequently than before; Fletcher became his successor as chief dramatist for the King's company. In these years they appear to have collaborated in *The Two Noble Kinsmen, Henry VIII,* and probably in the lost *Cardenio.* Is it too fantastic to suppose that Shakespeare was at least an adviser in the preparation of *Philaster, A King and No King,* and *The Maid's Tragedy* for his fellows? Is it even more fantastic to think that Shakespeare, the old public theatre playwright, preparing his first and crucial play for a private theatre, might have asked advice—or even taken it—from the two young dramatists who had written plays for this theatre and audience four or five times before?

SHAKESPEARE AND THE BLACKFRIARS THEATRE

Perhaps this is going too far. I do not wish to close on a note of speculation. My basic contention is that Shakespeare was, throughout his career, a man of the theatre and a devoted member of the King's company. One of the most important events in the history of that company was its acquisition of the Blackfriars playhouse in 1608 and its subsequent brilliantly successful exploitation of the stage and audience. The company was experienced and theatre-wise; the most elementary theatrical foresight demanded that in 1608 they prepare new and different plays for a new and different theatre and audience. Shakespeare was their loved and trusted fellow. How could they fail to ask him for new Blackfriars plays, and how could he fail them? All the facts at our command seem to me to demonstrate that he did not fail them. He turned from his old and tested methods and produced a new kind of play for the new theatre and audience. Somewhat unsurely at first he wrote *Cymbeline* for them, then, with greater dexterity in his new medium, *The Winter's Tale,* and finally, triumphant in his old mastery, *The Tempest.*

V.

Shakespeare's Theatre and After

IN THE years after Shakespeare's retirement to Stratford, the old division in the London theatre audience, the division which is illustrated by Shakespeare's turn to the Blackfriars, developed into a schism which was of lasting and unhappy consequence. This schism, its characteristics, and its results are the subject of this chapter.

His audience is, of course, only one of the essential elements in the professional environment of a playwright. The other principal elements, the theatre buildings and the acting companies, did not change so radically in the reigns of James I and Charles I. The type of Elizabethan dramatic company which Shakespeare utilized so effectively in the first ten or fifteen years of the seventeenth century, remained essentially unchanged until the abolition by Parliament of all acting at the beginning of the Civil Wars in September 1642. The better companies became more prosperous and therefore larger; and in 1637 a new and successful boy company was established under the directorship of Christopher Beeston at the Phoenix. But the old system of casts designed for doubling in order to fit the size and the personnel of the troupe by which the play had been commissioned was just as basic to the design of the comedies and tragi-comedies of the leading Caroline dramatists, like James Shirley and Philip Massinger, as it had been to the plays of Elizabethan and Jacobean playwrights like Shakespeare and Heywood. Indeed, as we have seen, the prompt manuscript of Massinger's *Believe as You List,* licensed for performance in 1631, is one of the most explicit examples of the system.

Very different, however, was the state of affairs in the Caroline theatres, and especially in their audiences. In audiences there was a marked change in the generation which followed Shakespeare, a change which seems to me important in the history of the theatre, and one which has received little attention from historians.[1] A preliminary review of

[1] The most extensive study of the Elizabethan and early Jacobean audiences in the different types of London theatres

certain characteristics of Shakespeare's familiar Globe theatre and its audience may help to make clear the significance of the change which took place in London during the second, third, and fourth decades of the seventeenth century.

Most students know that the Globe was a large open-air theatre which, according to the repeated statements of the only contemporary to give an exact figure,[2] had a capacity of 3,000—an astonishing capacity when one notes that it is greater than that of the usual London or New York theatre today, and that this large Globe was always in successful competition with three to five other London playhouses. Students also know that the audience in this theatre was made up of all classes of London society, watching the same play at the same time—noblemen, courtiers, and ladies in the boxes or private rooms; merchants and their wives, lawyers,

is Alfred Harbage's *Shakespeare and the Rival Traditions* (New York, 1952). The book is not concerned, however, with the period after 1613, and, in my opinion, it tends to exaggerate the differences between the audiences in the earlier public and private theatres and to minimize the overlapping.

[2] The Spanish Ambassador in dispatches to Madrid. See Edward M. Wilson and Olga Turner, "The Spanish Protest against *A Game at Chesse*," *Modern Language Review*, XLIV (1949), 476–482.

doctors, country gentry, and foreign visitors in the galleries; artisans and sailors, hostlers and housemaids, beggars, watermen, carters, and butchers in the pit. And throughout the house there was a good sprinkling of professionals on duty who found the playhouse a good theatre of operations, namely pickpockets and whores.

This is the theatre and this is the audience that Shakespeare had in mind as he wrote *Julius Caesar* and *Othello, As You Like It* and *King Lear,* a theatre audience whose astonishing variety cannot be duplicated in the modern world and, so far as I know, has not been duplicated since the seventeenth century. The variety of classes, tastes, education, and backgrounds is a phenomenon of Shakespeare's time. The audience, together with the distinctive physical theatre of the Elizabethans, is a factor of great importance in making the plays of Marlowe and Shakespeare, Dekker and Webster what they were. The Elizabethan public theatres, with their unique facilities for achieving speed, intimacy of effect, and flexibility in the presentation of plays, provided Elizabethan dramatists with an essential element in their development. Most of Shakespeare's dramatic work—excepting, as I have tried to show, the plays of the last period—need to be visualized as they were performed in such a theatre before such an audience for a proper understanding of his art. His plays, as we noted at the beginning, are clearly not planned for the reader in his study.

These characteristics of Shakespeare's theatre as the setting and part of the impetus for the drama of his time are probably familiar to most students. When asked what *was* the period of the theatre of Shakespeare's time they would say, perhaps with some fumbling: "Well, from the building of the first London theatre in 1576 until the abolition of all theatres and acting by Parliament in 1642 at the beginning of the Civil War."

Now so far as the Elizabethan public theatre *buildings* are concerned, this is true. The public theatres shut down by law in 1642—the Globe, the Red Bull, and the Fortune—appear to have been much the same as the structure built in 1576 and called simply The Theatre. But the audience which attended these theatres in the 1630's and 1640's was not at all the same, and herein lies the great change.

For the Jacobean and Caroline audience that watched the plays of Shakespeare's immediate successors—John Fletcher or Philip Massinger or

James Shirley—was not the old representative cross-section of London. Before Charles I succeeded his father in 1625, there had developed two different kinds of audiences frequenting two different kinds of theatres and demanding two different kinds of plays. This division is important, because it became fundamental in our own theatre; it leads directly to the peculiar Restoration coterie theatre of Etherege, Wycherly, Dryden, and Congreve. In the eighteenth and nineteenth centuries the English and American theatre got over this exclusiveness, but though the audiences grew larger and certainly more vulgar, the theatre never regained the universal audience of Shakespeare's Globe. The audience that gave a man of genius such a magnificent opportunity to speak to his time in his plays has never appeared again in the commercial theatre; it was lost, apparently forever, in the reigns of James I and Charles I.

This great shift in the English theatre has interested me for a number of years. The seeds of change had begun to grow in Shakespeare's time, but it was not apparent what they were leading to until shortly after his death. During all Shakespeare's working years there were two kinds of theatres in London: the public theatres that we have noticed and that we think of as "Shakespeare's theatre" and the so-called private theatres like Blackfriars and St. Paul's and Whitefriars, in which the boy companies acted. Private theatres were always exclusive because their rates of admission were six times those of the public theatres; they were always small and enclosed; and they catered to an audience of gentry and sophisticates. But though they were always there, they were never dominant until after James I had been on the throne for a few years. The great majority of Shakespeare's plays are public theatre plays, and so are Marlowe's and Heywood's and Dekker's and the best of Webster's.

But after the death of Elizabeth the balance began to shift. The royal and courtly influence on the drama increased. Naturally the actors and the playwrights thought the growth in court patronage was a wonderful thing: it made them more respectable, and it made them richer—two great goods not always found in conjunction. Of course they liked to show off their abilities before royalty, the most distinguished of the nobility, and the diplomatic corps of London, all assembled in the Great Hall at Hampton Court or at Greenwich or at Whitehall. They enjoyed the fees they were paid for court performances, fees well in excess of their average take at the public theatres. And they enjoyed the advertising the company and their plays got because they had been exhibited before the glittering throng at the court of King James.

The evidence of this greatly increased interest of the Stuart court in the plays and in the dramatists is clear. Whereas Elizabeth in the last ten years of her reign had commanded players to court about six or seven times a year, James usually had command performances twenty and sometimes thirty times a year. Moreover, as soon as James came to the throne, the principal companies received the personal sponsorship of the royal family and became the King's company and Queen Anne's company and Prince Henry's company, and as such they wore royal livery.

This markedly increased interest of the royal family and the court in the players soon began to influence the professional activities of the London repertory companies. The most striking evidence of the new orientation is the decision of Shakespeare's company discussed in the last chapter—the 1608 decision to purchase the Blackfriars and to play in this private theatre instead of the Globe during the autumn and winter months when the court and many of the gentry were in town.

Such a transfer of acting companies from one theatre to another was a common occurrence; it had happened many times in the preceding thirty years. But this particular transfer was a totally different thing. Heretofore only boy companies had acted in private theatres. Adult companies (like the King's men) had always confined themselves to the public theatres, with their great capacity and their large mixed audiences. In 1608, for the first time in the history of the English theatre, a regular adult London company decided to try to attract the exclusive audience of the private theatre that had always been the clientele of boy companies. It was a very risky venture, and the company hedged its investment by continuing to play, during the warmer months of the year, at the Globe on the Bankside.

But like most of the ventures of the King's company of players, this one turned out to be a great success. Figures that we get twenty years later show that they were then taking twice as much money at the Blackfriars as at the much larger Globe. Though they continued to act at both theatres, they gradually came to be in the eyes of the public, as we have seen, the company of the Blackfriars, not of the Globe.

Not only did the King's company, the premier London troupe, become primarily a private theatre company in the Jacobean and Caroline period, but their success influenced the other leading companies to build new private theatres. When the King's men took over the Blackfriars, all the other leading companies in London were public theatre companies; early in the reign of King Charles not one of them was. The memorable plays of the later Jacobean and the Caroline period are the plays written for the private theatres, for the King's men at Blackfriars, for Lady Elizabeth's and Queen Henrietta's men at the Phoenix or Cockpit in Drury Lane, and for the King's Revels company at the Salisbury Court Theatre.

The old public theatres, however, had by no means gone out of business. The Globe, the Fortune, and the Red Bull still drew crowds, and they continued to do so until Parliament closed all theatres. But they were different crowds. Most of the public theatre plays do not get published at all in these later years; the allusions to theatrical affairs in the extant correspondence of the time seldom mention public theatres; the diarists like Sir Humphrey Mildmay and Lady Clifford and John Greene refer to Blackfriars and the Phoenix, not to the

Globe, the Fortune, or the Red Bull. The London theatre has become a *dual* institution: one theatre for the court, the gentry, and the literate, another theatre for the vulgar masses. At Blackfriars and the Phoenix and the Salisbury Court, people like the Mildmays and Lady Newport, the Duke of Lennox and Lord Digby, Sir John Suckling and Bulstrode Whitelocke watched the plays of Fletcher and Shirley and Davenant and Massinger; at the Red Bull and the Globe and the Fortune were the artisans and tradesmen, apprentices and sailors who (in the later years) made up the London mob that became such a problem as the country drew closer to civil war.

Now let me note three or four examples of the sort of activities characteristic of the two types of theatre that unfortunately developed in the Jacobean and Caroline period. The first example is a generalized account of the propensities of audiences at the Fortune and the Red Bull in the 1630's. The author is Edmund Gayton, who was writing in 1654 of his memory of events that had occurred twenty-five years or so before:

> I have heard (he said) that the poets of the Fortune and Red Bull had always a mouth measure for their actors (who were terrible tear throats)

and made their lines proportionable to their compass—which were sesquipedales, a foot and a half. [In a later passage he goes on to recount scenes and policies at these theatres.] If it be on holy days when sailors, watermen, shoemakers, butchers and apprentices are at leisure, then it is good policy to amaze those violent spirits with some tearing tragedy full of fights and skirmishes: as the *Guelphs and Ghiblins, Greeks and Trojans,* or the *Three London Apprentices,* which commonly ends in six acts, the spectators frequently mounting the stage, and making a more bloody Catastrophe amongst themselves, than the Players did. I have known upon one of these *Festivals,* but especially at *Shrove-tide,* where the Players have been appointed, notwithstanding their playbills to the contrary, to act what the major part of the company had a mind to; sometimes *Tamerlane,* sometimes *Jugurth,* sometimes *The Jew of Malta,* and sometimes parts of all these, and at last, none of the three taking, they were forced to undress and put off their Tragic habits, and conclude the day with *The Merry Milk-maides.*

And unless this were done, and the popular humor satisfied, as sometimes it so fortuned, that the Players were refractory, then the Benches, the tiles, the laths, the stones, Oranges, Apples, Nuts, flew about most liberally, and as there were Mechanicks of all professions, who fell every one to his own trade, they dissolved a house in an instant, and made a ruin of a stately Fabrick. It was not then the most mimicall nor fighting man, *Fowler,* nor *Andrew Cane* [who were principal actors at the Fortune and the Red Bull] could pacify; Prologues nor Epilogues would prevail; the Devil and the Fool were quite out of favour. Nothing but noise and tumult fills the house, untill a cogg take 'em, and then to the Bawdy houses, and reform them; and instantly to the Banks side, where the poor Bears must conclude the riot, and fight twenty dogs at a time beside the Butchers, which sometimes fell into the service; this performed, and the Horse and Jack-an-Apes for a jig, they had sport enough that day for nothing.[3]

While audiences at the Red Bull and the Fortune were enjoying such full participation in the drama, the Blackfriars audience was creating problems of another sort. Blackfriars was troubled with a traffic problem, which was dealt with by the Privy Council of the King, a body made up of national officials like the Lord Treasurer, the Lord Keeper of the Privy Seal, the Archbishop of York, the Archbishop of Canterbury, the Earl Marshall, and others of

[3] Edmund Gayton, *Pleasant Notes upon Don Quixote* (London, 1654), pp. 24, 271–272. Modernized.

similar importance. On 20 November 1633 the Privy Council issued an order entitled:

> About going to the Blackfriars Playhouse in Coaches.
>
> Whereas the Board has taken consideration of the great inconveniences that grow by reason of the resort to the playhouse of Blackfriars in Coaches, whereby the streets near thereunto are at the play time so stopped up that his Majesty's subjects going about their necessary affairs can hardly find passage and are oftentimes endangered. Their Lordships . . . do therefore order that if any person, man or woman, of what condition soever repair to the aforesaid playhouse in a coach, so soon as they are gone out of their Coaches the Coachmen shall depart thence and not return until the end of the play, nor shall stay or return to fetch those whom they carried any nearer with their Coaches than the further side of St. Paul's churchyard on the one side, and Fleet Street Conduit on the other side; and in the time between their departure and return shall either return home or else abide in some other streets less frequented with passengers and so range their Coaches in those places that the way be not stopped.[4]

[4] From the Privy Council Register, Charles I. Public

The audience at the Fortune and Red Bull that took part in the merry destruction described by Edmund Gayton had not come to the theatre in their coaches. But the character of the audience at Blackfriars is even more eloquently pictured by the second order issued by the Privy Council only five weeks after the first. Their Lordships had to eat their words. The second order says:

Touching the Playhouse in Blackfriars.

Upon information this day given to the Board of the discomodity that divers persons of great quality, especially Ladies and Gentlewomen, did receive in going to the Playhouse of Blackfriars, by reason that no Coaches may stand within the Blackfriars Gate or return thither during the play. ... The Board taking into consideration the former order of 20 November last concerning this business did think fit to explain the said order in such manner that as many Coaches as may stand within Blackfriars Gate may enter and stay there or return thither at the end of the play, but that the said former order of 20 November be duly observed in all other parts.[5]

Record Office, London. Reprinted in the *Malone Society Collections,* I, Parts iv, v (1911), 387–388. Spelling and punctuation have been modernized.
[5] *Ibid.,* pp. 388–389.

Even these ladies and gentlewomen who were influential enough to get a Privy Council order amended when the parking restrictions displeased them were not the most distinguished patrons of Blackfriars. When Charles Louis, Prince of the Palatinate, was visiting his uncle, King Charles, in 1636, he wrote home to his mother, the Queen of Bohemia, about visiting the studio of Anthony Van Dyke, who at this time was painting so many of his famous portraits of English court figures, and he spoke of the picture of King Charles that Van Dyke was then painting for her:

> The King sat yesterday at Van Dyke's . . . his house is close by Blackfriars, where the Queen saw Lodowick Carlell's second part of Arviragus and Felicia acted, which is hugely liked of every one. . . .[6]

This extraordinary visit of Queen Henrietta Maria to the private theatre of the King's men is only one of four different occasions on which she is known to have seen a performance at that playhouse. Of course Henrietta Maria was a frivolous Frenchwoman who was once severely criticized for par-

[6] *Historical Manuscripts Commission.* Northumberland Manuscripts. Appendix to the Third Report, p. 118, No. 132.

ticipating in an amateur performance in her own palace—she was young, and perhaps may be forgiven for light spirits. She did not stretch decorum, however, by visiting any other theatre, even that of her own company, and certainly she did not go to any of the public theatres where her less cultivated subjects flocked in throngs.

How much less cultivated these other subjects were is indicated by a mob action of eight years before, which began with the audience of the Fortune theatre. At the time of this mob action the Duke of Buckingham was probably the most widely hated man in all England, so widely hated that when he was assassinated two years later there was public rejoicing. The fear and hatred of Buckingham were, of course, extended to many of his associates, one of whom was Dr. Lamb, a quack doctor and necromancer who was popularly believed to have instigated the Duke in poisoning plots and to have furnished him with love potions for his amorous adventures. There are several contemporary accounts of Dr. Lamb's last visit to the Fortune theatre.

> Upon Friday being the 13th of June . . . he went to see a play at the Fortune [theatre] where the boys of the town and other unruly people having

observed him present, after the play was ended, flocked about him and began to quarrel with and affront him, calling him the duke's devil, and in such sort, that he hired some sailors and others that he gathered up to guard him home. He came in at Moorgate, and the people following him. He supped at a cook's shop, where the people watched him, whilst his guard defended him from their violence. Thence he goes to the Windmill Tavern, in Lothbury, the tumult still increasing. At length, as he came thence, the people set upon him. He flies to another house, where they threw stones, and threatened to pull down the house, unless Lamb were delivered to them. The master of the house, a lawyer, fearing what might ensue, wisely sends for four constables to guard him out of his house. But the rage of the people so much increased (no man can tell why or for what cause) that in the midst of these auxiliaries they struck him down to the ground, giving him divers blows and wounds, and quite beat out one of his eyes. Thus being left half dead, and in such a case, that he never spoke after, he was carried to the Compter, in the Poultry (no other house being willing to receive him) where the next morning he ended a wretched life by a miserable and strange [death]. Some say, the keeper got above £20 by taking twopence a groat apiece of such as came to see him when he was dead.[7]

This lynching of Dr. Lamb is one of the more horrible examples of London mob action in the time, but mobs were not peculiar to the Fortune among the public theatres. Only four weeks earlier in the same season a mob at the Globe theatre had been forestalled. It was foiled by an order that the Privy Council sent to all justices of the peace in Surrey—the county in which the Globe stood. Their Lordships wrote:

> Whereas we are informed that on Thursday next divers loose and idle persons, some sailors, and others have appointed to meet at the playhouse called the Globe to see a play (as it is pretended) but their end is thereby to disguise some routous and riotous action. We have therefore thought fit to give you notice of the information which we have received concerning this their purpose. And we do likewise hereby will and require you to take very careful and strict order that *no play be acted*

[7] Letter of Joseph Mead to Sir Martin Stuteville. Thomas Birch, *The Court and Times of Charles the First* (2 vols.; London, 1848), I, 364–365. Supplemented from *A Briefe Description of the Notorious Life of Iohn Lambe otherwise called Doctor Lambe. Together with his Ignominious Death* (Amsterdam, 1628).

on that day, and also to have that strength about you as you shall think sufficient for the suppression of any insolencies or other mutinous intentions....[8]

Riots and lynchings at the Globe and the Fortune, ladies in their coaches and Queen Henrietta Maria at the Blackfriars: this is a violent contrast in audiences, really too violent, for at the private theatres all was not peace and respectful attention by any means. A little consideration of the disturbers of the peace at Blackfriars may bring the contrast into more accurate focus, but note how different the rows at Blackfriars were from the rows at the Fortune or the Red Bull or the Globe.

In May 1635 the London correspondent of Viscount Wentworth wrote to him that

The quarrel that lately broke out betwixt my Lord Digby and Will Crofts in the Blackfriars at a play stands as it did when your brother went hence. Crofts stands confined to his father's house because by striking he broke his bonds of £5,000. But there was a great difference in the parties that stood bound [for the two opponents]: my Lord

[8] From the Privy Council Register, Charles I. Public Record Office, London. Reprinted in the *Malone Society Collections,* I, Parts iv, v (1911), 382. Spelling and punctuation modernized.

Bedford and Sir John Strangwick stipulated for my Lord Digby, Tom Eliot and Jack Crofts, men of small fortunes, for the other, that they should keep the peace during the suit depending in the Star Chamber. The Lords have heard it and reported their opinions to the King and there it rests.[9]

This fight in the theatre cannot have been very flattering to the actors on the stage, but the personages involved were far different from the rioters at the Globe. George Digby was the son and heir of the Earl of Bristol—Van Dyke painted a fine portrait of him about this time, and a few years later he was an eloquent and courageous defender of the Earl of Strafford before the House of Commons. Will Crofts was a courtier in the service of the Queen. Their trial was heard, not by Justices of the Peace, but by the Lords of the Star Chamber, who submitted their findings for ratification to the King.

About eight months after this dust-up in the Blackfriars, another letter from a London correspondent recounts a difference of opinion directly

[9] William Knowler, ed., *The Earle of Strafforde's Letters and Dispatches* (2 vols.; London, 1739), I, 426. Spelling and punctuation modernized.

concerned with the theatre. The letter says,

> A little pique happened betwixt the Duke of Lennox and the Lord Chamberlain about a box at a new play in the Blackfriars, of which the Duke had got the key. Which if it had come to be debated betwixt them, as it was once intended, some heat or perhaps other inconvenience might have happened. His Majesty, hearing of it, sent the Earl of Holland to command them both not to dispute it [except in his presence]. So he heard [the dispute] and made them friends [again].[10]

These two squabblers over a box at the Blackfriars were even more exalted personages than Digby and Crofts. The Lord Chamberlain was the Earl of Pembroke and Montgomery; to him and to his brother the First Folio of Shakespeare's works had been dedicated in 1623. In his office as Lord Chamberlain he was in charge of all entertainments of any kind that took place at royal palaces; he had more patronage to dispense than almost any other nobleman, and he was the official of highest appeal for all actors and playwrights in London. Very few persons would have dared to dispute with the Earl of Pembroke and Montgomery, especially over theatrical affairs. But the Duke of Lennox outranked

[10] *Ibid.*, p. 511. Modernized.

him in the peerage; besides, he was the King's cousin and one of his especial favorites.

These petty quarrels of the principal noblemen of the realm at Blackfriars and the carrying of their disputes from the playhouse to the King sound very much like the affairs of the Restoration theatre. It is precisely the sort of thing that was going on in the 1660's and 1670's when King Charles II intervened to smooth out the rows of Rochester and Sedley and Buckingham, and Nell Gwynne and Moll Davis and the Duchess of Castlemaine at Drury Lane or Lincoln's Inn Fields. This intimate association between the theatre, its coterie audience, and the court and the crown is generally thought of as peculiar to the Restoration theatre, but it had begun in London long before.

The peculiar character of a coterie audience made up of individuals of similar status and tastes and well known to one another is also suggested at the Blackfriars by another theatrical reminiscence. This one is written by Bulstrode Whitelocke, a fairly prominent political figure who generally spoke on the Puritan side in the debates in the House of Commons and who held various offices under the Parliamentary government after 1642. The tone of his reminiscences is set by the fact that he wrote them for his children; he is therefore concerned to make himself appear a moral and upright young man; consequently he plays down the frequency of his visits to Blackfriars. Whitelocke said to his children:

> I was so conversant with the musicians, and so willing to gain their favor, especially at this time, that I composed an air myself, with the assistance of Mr. Ives, and called it *Whitelocke's Coranto*; which being cried up, was first played publicly by the Blackfriars Music, who were then esteemed the best of common musicians in London. Whenever I came to that house (as I did sometimes in those days) though not often, to see a play, the musicians would presently play *Whitelocke's Coranto*, and it was so often called for that they would have played it twice or thrice in an afternoon.[11]

The fact that the musicians of the Blackfriars orchestra knew the patrons of the house well enough to recognize them and play their compositions when they entered is a good measure of the

---

[11] "Whitelocke's labours remembered in the annales of his life, written for the use of his children, MS." Printed in Charles Burney, *A General History of Music*, ed. Frank Mercer (2 vols.; London, 1935), II, 299. Spelling and punctuation modernized.

homogenous character of the private theatre audience of the reign of Charles I.

It is fairly obvious that audiences as different as those we have noticed at the Red Bull, the Fortune, and the Globe on the one hand, and at the private theatres like the Blackfriars on the other, must have required different kinds of plays. Of course the actors and the playwrights were conscious of this fact and as a consequence prepared for the Blackfriars and the Phoenix pieces like Carlell's *Arviragus and Philicia,* Davenant's *Love and Honor,* Fletcher's *The Wild Goose Chase,* and Shirley's *The Lady of Pleasure.* For the public theatres they prepared plays like *The Whore New Vamped, The Knave in Grain, The Valiant Scot,* and *The Late Murder of the Son upon the Mother, or Keep the Widow Waking.*

But sometimes there was confusion, and a public theatre put on a play which had been written for a private theatre. This was a particular risk for the King's company, which ran both the Globe and the Blackfriars and used the same actors at each. On one occasion (for reasons now unknown) they had to present at the Globe a play by James Shirley called *The Doubtful Heir,* which, as Shirley himself said when he published it, "should have been presented at the Blackfriars." Shirley wrote a prologue for the production in which he tried to prepare the Globe audience for the unfamiliar type of play they were about to see. One has some sympathy for the actor who had to come down stage in the midst of a Globe audience in the summer of 1640 and deliver the following lines:

> All that the Prologue comes for, is to say,
> Our Author did not calculate this Play
> For this Meridian; the Banckside, he knows,
> Are far more skilfull at the Ebbes and flows
> Of water, than of wit; he did not mean
> For the elevation of your poles, this scene.
> No shews, no dance, and what you most delight in,
> Grave understanders, here's no target fighting
> Upon the Stage, all work for Cutlers barr'd,
> No bawdery, nor no Ballets; this goes hard;
> But language clean, and what affects you not,
> Without impossibilities the Plot;
> No clown, no squibs, no Devill in't; oh now
> You Squirrels that want Nuts, what will you do?
> Pray do not crack the benches; and we may
> Hereafter fit your Palats with a Play:
> But you that can contract your selves, and sit
> As you were now in the *Black-Fryers* pit;
> And will not deaf us, with leud noise and tongues,
> Because we have no Heart to break our Lungs,

Will pardon our vast Stage, and not disgrace
This Play, meant for your persons, not the place.

How the actor who read this insulting prologue to a rowdy Globe audience escaped without being chased out of the theatre, I do not understand.

The two theatre audiences so clearly distinguished by James Shirley in his prologue for *The Doubtful Heir* are characteristic of the Jacobean and Caroline period. Shakespeare's universal audience of forty years before at the same playhouse had disappeared forever. When theatrical productions were resumed in London at the Restoration of Charles II, after eighteen years of dark theatres, only the private theatre audience had survived. Even that audience had shrunk, for though Caroline London supported three private theatres (as well as the three public ones) Restoration London could just barely support two.

The fixation of this unhappy division of the theatre's patrons into a vulgar group and an aristocratic group can, I think, be traced to the establishment by Shakespeare and his Fellows of the King's company in 1608 of a *dual* audience for their productions: a coterie theatre in Blackfriars and a theatre for the masses in the Globe. What had previously been fortuitous and occasional became, through their ingenious operation of two theatres with the same troupe of actors, deliberate and customary. No doubt their new scheme was well intentioned, and the history of the company for the next thirty-four years shows that it was certainly profitable. For the development of English theatre and drama in the last three and one half centuries, however, it has proved to be not only a turning point, but perhaps a point of no return.